W9-BVE-790

"In typical Gregoire style, Sheila addresses a delicate issue with clarity, grace, and humor. *Honey, I Don't Have a Headache Tonight* will make a lot of husbands very happy . . . and their wives too!"

—Dr. Scott Turansky
Cofounder, the National Center for Biblical Parenting
Author of *Say Goodbye to Whining, Complaining, and
Bad Attitudes in You and Your Kids*

"Sheila Wray Gregoire is hopeful, helpful, honest, and hilarious as she uncovers and offers solutions for the real problems married couples face in the bedroom. When it comes to sexual intimacy, *Honey, I Don't Have a Headache Tonight* is one of the most powerful and practical books on the market today."

—Ginger Plowman
Speaker and author of *Don't Make Me Count to Three!*

"*Honey, I Don't Have a Headache Tonight* is more than a catchy title. It offers practical, insightful help for any couple wanting to improve emotional and sexual intimacy and should be recommended reading for any young couple preparing for marriage. Sheila's wit allows her to tackle a sensitive subject in a way that invites couples to explore their own hang-ups and obstacles to a rich and rewarding sex life and points them toward marriage as God intended it to be."

—Denise MacDonald, M.Div.
Therapist, Family Works Counselling

honey,
i don't
have a
headache
tonight

honey,
i don't
have a
headache
tonight

Help for Women Who Want to
Feel More "In the Mood"

sheila wray gregoire

Kregel
Publications

Honey, I Don't Have a Headache Tonight: Help for Women Who Want to Feel More "In the Mood"

© 2004 by Sheila Wray Gregoire

Published by Kregel Publications, a division of Kregel, Inc., P.O. Box 2607, Grand Rapids, MI 49501.

All rights reserved. No part of this book may be reproduced, stored in a retrieval system, or transmitted in any form or by any means—electronic, mechanical, photocopy, recording, or otherwise—without written permission of the publisher, except for brief quotations in printed reviews.

All Scripture quotations are from the *Holy Bible, New International Version®*. © 1973, 1978, 1984 by International Bible Society. Used by permission of Zondervan Publishing House. All rights reserved.

This book is not intended to take the place of legal, medical, or psychological counsel or treatment. If assistance in any of these areas is needed, please seek the services of a certified professional.

Cover design: John M. Lucas

Library of Congress Cataloging-in-Publication Data
Gregoire, Sheila Wray.
    Honey, I don't have a headache tonight: help for women who want to feel more "in the mood" / by Sheila Wray Gregoire.
        p. cm.
Includes bibliographical references.
    1. Sex—Religious aspects—Christianity. 2. Sex in marriage—Religious aspects—Christianity. 3. Wives—Sexual behavior. 4. Marriage—Religious aspects—Christianity. I. Title.
BT708.G715   2004
248.8'435—dc21   2004009067

ISBN 0-8254-2693-6

Printed in the United States of America

OVERTON MEMORIAL LIBRARY 04 05 06 07 08 / 5 4 3 2
HERITAGE CHRISTIAN UNIVERSITY
P.O. Box HCU
Florence, Alabama 35630

To Susan, Jill, Karen, Lori, and Janet,
who were my sounding boards as we laughed
in the van riding up to Muskoka Baptist Conference
when this book was born.

Contents

Foreword

I have some friends who are in the middle of rehabbing a house. During the day they go to their full-time jobs, and in the evenings they strip wallpaper, wash windows, and pull up old carpeting. By the time they get home, they're pooped, which doesn't leave much room for intimacy. Realistically, it barely leaves room for grabbing supper, doing the laundry, paying the bills, and attending to all the other have-to's.

So last Saturday, after a full day of rehabbing, this couple went home, took showers, and mentioned to each other how exhausted they were. Imagine her surprise when her husband gave her "the look." You know "the look": those eyes that say, *Hey, Baby, I'm in the mood to make you crazy with passion. How about we take this to the bedroom?*

"I thought you were tired," she told him, trying not to sound overly shocked by his sudden burst of energy. "Plus, my whole body is sore." She scrolled through her mental files of what other excuses would be appropriate without hurting his ego.

Have you ever felt that way?

You want to have sex. You distantly remember that you *used* to enjoy sex. But now the bed seems to call you for another reason: namely, to sleep.

Between kids, a job, housework, church and community obligations, family ties, and everything else under the sun, sex drops to the bottom of the "to-do" list—if it makes it there at all. Not exactly romantic. And not something that nominates you for the Nobel Peace Prize, in your husband's estimation.

So what did my friend do last Saturday?

Well, she had a brief, but serious, conversation with herself (all in her head, of course) in which she weighed her options and the subsequent consequences. Then she did what Sheila recommends in this book you're holding. She said "yes" to her husband.

She pushed everything else out of her mind, to be "in the moment." And the most amazing things happened. Not only did she get "in the mood," it drew her closer to her spouse, she had fun, and it helped her sleep better. And the next day, her husband worked like a superhero around their house and at the rehabbing house!

"All I can say is, 'Wahoo!'" my friend told me (and, by the way, she also gave me permission to share this story). "I just wish I could remember all those benefits when my mind is saying, *No, no, no. Stay away from me!*"

I know I've felt that way. While I love the physical aspect of sex when I say "yes" to my husband, what I really love is how it makes me feel emotionally, relationally, and even spiritually. There's something amazing that happens to my marriage and my faith in those moments of intimacy.

But, admittedly, there are times when I just don't even care about the amazing benefits of sex. Sometimes I'm just "too pooped to whoop," to borrow a phrase from Christian psychologist Dr. Kevin Leman.

If you find yourself in that same place, you're holding the right book. In so many marriages, sex can be a source of tension, frustration, anxiety, stress, and conflict. But Sheila shows us that sex doesn't have to be that way. With biblical insight, sensitivity, hope, and even some humor, she challenges women to view sex in a different light— a positive light filled with great benefits, both personally and relationally.

As managing editor of *Marriage Partnership* magazine I receive thousands of letters from frustrated wives who are tired of being harassed about sex. It's nice to have a resource I can recommend that is honest, forthright, and non-guilt-inducing.

If you want to overcome the obstacles that keep your sex-drive low—whether it's your body image, your busy lifestyle, your need for respect, or your past—you aren't alone . . . and there's hope. Don't give up yet! You've taken a first courageous step by reading Sheila's book. The rest of your marriage intimacy story is filled with promise.

—GINGER KOLBABA

Acknowledgments

The women of Parkdale Baptist Church in Belleville, Ontario have spent the last four months avoiding me. Everybody knew I was writing a book on sex, so as soon as church ended, they parted like the Red Sea in front of me.

When I did manage to snag some friends and ask them questions, I received some very interesting answers, from snickers and silence to "use chocolate body paint!" announced very loudly at the front of our sanctuary. To all the women I embarrassed, and to the many more I could not, I thank you for sharing your stories, either through e-mails or in person. I know it was not easy, but the stories make this book so much richer. I also very much appreciate those at Pioneer Camp who laughed with me until midnight, swapping sex challenges and solutions (and especially for the story of the migrating breasts).

I also want to thank my husband, Keith, whose permission I made sure I had before embarking on this quest. After all, it's one thing to write a book about parenting. It's quite another to write a book about sex. He didn't want to be at the front of the church, or attending the delivery of some baby in our hometown, only to have people thinking, *I know what you did, ha ha ha ha*. So I didn't include anything in this book about us that I thought was too personal. My very great gratitude for Keith, too, for the sacrifices he made in his work schedule to give me more writing time. He is the most supportive husband I could imagine.

I am indebted to my aunt, Alison Froese, who introduced me to Leanne Payne's work years ago. Her books shaped much of my thinking on sexual identities, healing, and wholeness.

Many thanks to Susan Douglas, Karen Dorey, Lisa Wood, and, as always, my mother Elizabeth Wray and mother-in-law Cheryl Gregoire, who looked after my girls on countless occasions when I was trying to "just finish up." Their encouragement in words and deeds made my life much easier (and my girls' lives much less boring).

To all those at Kregel, and especially to Dennis Hillman, thank you so much for believing in me for my first book and trusting me with this one as well. You are a wonderful, encouraging bunch of people with whom to work. Thanks to Stephen Barclift and Cheryl Dunlop, for editing; and to tireless Janyre Tromp, for quick answers to a myriad of questions, many of which didn't even relate to her field. To Janet Kobobel Grant, my agent, thanks for pursuing this project for me.

To my daughters, Becca and Katie, thanks for all the kisses and hugs and for letting Mommy work when I needed to. I am still trying to figure out how I will explain this book to you. You know all about *To Love, Honor, and Vacuum.* What will you think of this? Perhaps it's time to have that talk after all. . . .

And finally, I rejoice that we have such a wonderful Savior, who can heal our pasts and make us new, like a gleaming white bride, even in this most personal area of our lives. How amazing that He made husbands and wives to fit together in this way, and that through this union, when we're celebrating our love together, children can also be made. My prayer is that as women read this book, God can use it to free up their sexuality, letting everyone experience true love while making love, with a good dose of fun and laughter, too. May this help us to strengthen and build great marriages that will withstand anything and help keep our society from crumbling.

God bless you.

Introduction

M ost of us agree that sex is fun. But, then, chocolate is great too, and eating it in a candlelit bubble bath is awfully relaxing at the end of the day when kids have been vomiting, the washing machine broke again, or teenagers have been sulking.

While sex may be wonderful, for many women it's not always worth the effort. And unlike our dear spouses, for us it *is* an effort. We don't automatically get "in the mood." When we glimpse our darlings getting undressed, "hubba hubba" doesn't usually come to mind. Instead, we watch him shedding his clothes and think, *I hope he's not going to leave that laundry there for me.* We need to have our to-do lists ready, make sure everyone has something to wear tomorrow, and get the house somewhat livable before we even entertain the possibility of making love. To us, you see, making love is essentially a brain thing. We have to be in the right mood before it can be fun, but too many things conspire to rob us of that mood.

So what do we do? We try desperately hard to make sure our husbands don't get "in the mood" either, which is a losing proposition since most of them could be in the mood even if they have a temperature of 104 degrees and a rash all over. Nothing distracts them from the task at hand.

Nevertheless, we persevere. See if you can relate to Andrea.

Andrea's Evening of Evasion

It's 10:30 at night, the baby is finally settled, the older children are in bed, and Andrea just finished picking up the toys and clothes from the stairs after washing the dishes and feeding the pets. She throws a quick load of laundry into the dryer so her oldest can go to school tomorrow in something that matches. All she wants now, more than anything else, is to collapse into bed between those sheets—and sleep!

She climbs the stairs, heads down the hallway into the bedroom . . . and there's Jeff, waiting for her with that look in his eye. Andrea knows that the evasion pattern must now begin. She gives him a quick kiss on the cheek, moans to demonstrate how exhausted she is, and begins the litany of things she has to do tomorrow, in the hope that Jeff will understand that she's not rejecting him, she just wants rest. In the meantime, perhaps hearing her complain will distract him from his primary aim tonight.

Romance, you see, is the furthest thing from Andrea's mind. This man who was waiting for her in the bedroom didn't help when the kids were fighting tonight, except to yell, "You better stop that right now!" in a voice loud enough to rock the foundations of the house. He didn't help with the dishes even when the baby was crying to be held at the same time. (Andrea's getting to be a pro at doing dishes with one hand.) Instead, he retreated into the study to go over some papers before turning on the game. He did tuck the kids in, but only after Andrea gave them a bath. Frankly, she just isn't feeling too close to him at the moment.

So she throws on the largest flannel nightgown she can find and climbs under the covers. Undaunted, he crawls in beside her and hugs her, hoping for something more. And now, the crucial moment is at hand. He wants to start kissing. She wants to start snoring. But how does she let him down without starting a fight? She's really not energetic enough for one tonight.

"I'm just really tired, honey, okay? It's not that I don't love you, I just really need some sleep," Andrea says as she rolls over. Jeff doesn't say anything, but a few minutes later he lets out a long sigh and gets out of bed. Andrea wonders if he expects her to follow him to find out what's wrong. She knows the routine; they've been through it so many times before. If she doesn't go out there, Jeff will stay awake until 2:00 in the morning and be angry with her tomorrow. But if she goes out there, they'll end up endlessly discussing their sex life, get in a big fight, she likely won't get to sleep for at least two hours, and they'll both be mad all day tomorrow anyway. Which is worse? She votes for sleep now and recriminations later.

As she drifts off, without her husband next to her, she thinks that what really bothers her is that she always has to plan how to get him "turned off." She never even has time to figure out if *she* wants to be "turned on," because he always is. And she knows how miserable life is if she has to reject him outright, so she always has to try to give him the impression that she's not interested so that he never propositions her in the first place. The worst thing is if she kisses him too much when he gets home and he takes that as a sign that she's interested in something tonight. Then he's even angrier if she's too tired, and their relationship is that much worse.

She loves Jeff, but she's tired of these games. She wishes he would leave her alone and give her some space. Before the kids came, she really did enjoy sex, but now it's just one more thing she has to do. She doesn't like that. She misses the intimacy.

When they do make love, their relationship is so much better for a few days. Jeff even looks at the kids differently and actually helps around the house. But it's still not that easy for Andrea to get in the mood.

He can't seem to lower his sex drive, though, so the only thing that could help is if she makes hers higher. Frankly, with the kids, the laundry, and the dogs, that seems like a very remote possibility. She sighs, thinking about how distant she and her husband have become, and worries that the gulf can't be bridged. But mostly she's just angry. Angry at him for not understanding, and angry that he doesn't try to do anything to get her in the mood, other than ambush her at 10:30 at night with embraces that would have been far more welcome earlier, especially if they were followed by giving the kids a bath or even running one for *her* while he put the baby to bed for a change.

But change isn't in their future. Maybe when the kids get older. Maybe . . . but she drifts off. The last thing she hears is Jeff switching on the TV.

Men and Women Are Different

Andrea and Jeff have totally different perspectives on sex largely because men and women are simply different. We all know that, and it's a source of great frustration on the part of both spouses. Women wonder why men were created with the switch always turned on, and men wonder why women were created with so many different switches and no instruction manual.

And when sex conflicts enter a marriage, heartache soon follows because sex is so closely related to love. When women don't want sex, men can feel unloved, even if we women don't understand why. And women feel taken for granted and disrespected when men seem "sex crazy," even if that's not what our husbands intended. This is, of course, a generalization, for one-third of all women actually suffer from the opposite problem: their husbands aren't as interested in sex as they are.[1] Yet whenever extreme differences in sex drives enter a marriage, maintaining intimacy can be difficult.

A strong marriage is the foundation in a storm: the support that you need when your children are challenging, work is frustrating, or friendships are fleeting. Since sex is such a huge part of marriage and has so many emotional repercussions, it's a serious subject that needs to be addressed, even if it causes many snickers, downcast eyes, or, more likely, *Saturday Night Live*-type jokes.

Yet many books that talk about sex problems talk about *how to do it better*. In the Christian world, they help us understand our bodies better (many of us enter marriage with little knowledge of how sex works) and how to give each other pleasure. Secular books are often more risqué, listing new positions to use and new techniques to try (as if anything new can possibly be discovered). They suggest what scented candles to employ, what lingerie to buy, what toys will enhance everyone's pleasure. The focus, in both cases, is on *technique*.

Technique certainly can be important, and if you've never been able to physically enjoy sex, these books will likely prove very helpful.[2] Most of the women I've talked to, though, do not list technique as their primary problem. We know how to do it; most of us even enjoy it when we do. We just don't want to very often.

Many of us can relate to this popular joke: A couple walks in to see a marriage therapist, and she asks them how often they have sex. The husband says, "Hardly at all. Maybe two or three times a week." The wife replies, "All the time! He's all over me! Maybe two or three times a week." Our frames of reference are so different that it seems like a hopeless case. This book is primarily for those women who feel like their husbands are "all over them." We'll look at how we can make our sexual relationships—and thus our marriages—mutually satisfying. If you, on the other hand, look at those women who complain about their randy husbands with envy because you wish your husband had even an ounce of their appetites, you, too, can find some help here. As we'll see, sex is multifaceted. Change in the sexual relationship requires change elsewhere, whether or not you are the one living in the sexual desert.

Most of us who yearn for a lower-stress sex life, though, are left with only two possible solutions: get our husbands to want it *less* (okay, okay, stop laughing so hard), or get *us* to want it *more*. I know that the latter seems almost impossible, but it's the only option we can directly affect. All the flannel nightgowns in the world aren't going to make his sex drive disappear—it's part of him. So, whether we like it or not, the ball's in our court.

But now that we have the ball, what do we do with it? Quite frankly, when I began writing this book, I didn't have the foggiest idea either. Why don't you join this research project with me, and in the process we can all learn how to make great marriages.

For Him

Even if you didn't personally buy this book for your wife, you're still probably down on your knees thanking God that she now owns a copy!

But I don't want you to be left out of the process. You may not feel like reading the whole book, so at the end of each chapter I'm going to summarize what your wife has read and make some suggestions for you, too.

I'd encourage you to actually read all of this introduction, though. It's not long, and maybe Andrea's story will help you gain some insight into what your wife is feeling. (Don't worry, you're going to get equal hearing later!)

Chapter 1

He's an Alien

I'm going to start this book with a challenge: let's not settle for enough sex so that our husbands stop bugging us. Let's get the whole works. Imagine you and your husband enjoying a truly intimate, satisfying relationship, with both of you willing and eager to make love. It may sound impossible, but let's think of that as our potential.

In other words, let's not make improving your sex life an exercise you have to do grudgingly to make your marriage better. That hardly sounds fun, and it sure isn't going to inspire very many amorous thoughts. Instead, let it be an exciting adventure! You don't have to understand now how you're going to get there; just dream that it can happen. After all, what have you got to lose? Let's get excited—if you'll excuse the pun—about the prospect, and imagine what our lives could be like if all these relationship dreams came true.

But before we delve too deeply into this topic, relax! Often we take sex far too seriously. After all, if you think about it, sex more closely resembles a big cosmic joke than it does anything else. Our bodies are actually quite gross with all the different fluids and odors they produce. And what can be sillier than sex, where your desire is determined far more by the state of your house, your grocery list, or your children than by the state of your beloved? C. S. Lewis wrote that he was fairly certain God didn't mean for sex to be perfectly serious.[1] He meant it to reveal all our flaws, and yet also to help us accept each other nonetheless, just as God accepts us. It isn't meant to always be a perfectly mystical union, but instead meant to show grace and, perhaps even more frequently, God's sense of humor.

"Banish play and laughter from the bed of love and you may let in a false goddess," Lewis warns.[2] Take sex too seriously and you risk losing love altogether. So laugh a little with God, and commit this area of your life to Him. You can do it.

We Have Different Sex Drives

Many people believe the sexes are not essentially different (they think we're just raised to be different), but when sex drives come into the picture, it's not hard to prove the case. Why do so many men frequent strip joints and buy *Playboy? Playgirl* has a much smaller readership (and many readers are actually gay men).[3] Most women don't get turned on by a flip of a switch.

Roy Baumeister and his colleagues surveyed the psychological literature regarding sex drives and concluded that men's sex drives tend to be more "fixed, urgent, and biologically driven," whereas women's sex drives are more "fluid, flexible, and influenced by social settings."[4] In other words, men's sex drives arise from the urgency their bodies feel, whereas women's sex drives arise more from their relationships. Although we can enjoy sex as much as men can, it won't meet all of our needs. It may temporarily feel nice and help us to feel closer to our husbands, but that's not our primary emotional need. Instead, we want to feel loved, and, ironically, sex doesn't always provide that.

Yet relationship worries aren't the only things that can jeopardize our sex lives. You could be warming up with some loving kisses when you suddenly remember, with stark panic, that your teenager needs an application for a college scholarship filled out by tomorrow, and you're not sure if she has finished it or not. Or that you promised to carpool your daughter to gymnastics this week, but your son has to stay after school to practice for a play, and you don't know how you can pick up two children at different parts of the city at the same time. Sometimes it's something far more mundane, such as realizing you need to go grocery shopping, and then starting to tick off in your mind what should be on the list. We don't mean to think about these things; they just pop into our heads, and before we know it we're no longer concentrating on our husbands. And when we do this, our ability to physically respond gets turned off.

Think about our different responses to headaches. When a woman has a headache, she can't have sex. The pain is stopping her from concentrating on pleasure. Even the flu, though, is not enough to keep many men from being interested in sex, something that causes new brides no end of incredulity. We can't picture ourselves ever being ready, let alone eager, for sex when we're sick, so how can he?

It's All in Your Head

At this point many of you are probably waiting on the edge of your seat because you are ready to start talking about sex. I'm sorry to say you're going to have to wait awhile, because we aren't even going to get to the logistics of sex for several chapters. No matter how tense a topic this may be in your marriage, unless you have a health condition that lowers your sex drive, sex is not your primary problem. That's because, as we've seen, for women sex is a "head thing." We have to sort out what's going on up there before we can move further south.

Some of us, though, do suffer from physical conditions that can lower desire, such as diabetes, anemia, arthritis, thyroid problems, or angina. Some medications, including the birth control pill, can also kill our libidos. If you believe your lack of desire may have a medical component, ask your doctor for advice on how you can cope in the meantime. Other women have specifically sexual problems, like vaginismus (pain during intercourse) or even pain during orgasm. Usually these have psychological roots, and talking to a Christian therapist may prove helpful.[5] Finally, a few of us truly do have nonexistent sex drives because of lower testosterone levels (both for men and women, testosterone fires us up). New medications can counteract this, so speak with your doctor if you suspect this may be the case.

Other physical conditions affect our sex drive, too, but there's nothing we can do medically because they're perfectly normal. Hormonal changes, menopause, pregnancy, and childbirth all affect our libidos, and we'll deal later in the book with how to cope with these things that all of us, to varying degrees, will face.

But most of us don't have medical problems. We just aren't as interested as our hubbies. It would actually be easier if our lower sex drive *was* due to some medical problem—like lower testosterone—because then there could be a quick solution. My husband is a pediatrician, and he frequently finds himself sitting across from desperate parents who want pills to control their hyperactive children. In many cases, though, the problem is not medical but behavioral. There is no quick fix.

That's where we women find ourselves, too. There is no pill we can pop to cure ourselves, much as we might like one. That's because there's nothing wrong with us if we don't want sex as much as our husbands do; we were created that way. Our problem is not that he can't "turn us on"; it's just that we don't always want him to. And the reason is because "it's all in our heads."

It's All in His Eyes

Though we may instinctively understand how women work, many of us feel completely blindsided by the way our husbands do. I remember as a teenager dressing without giving any thought to what effect it would have on hormone-raging seventeen-year-old boys whose thoughts turn to sex about every 2.3 seconds. My eyes were opened when I was married and Keith would comment favorably on some outfit I had once worn. I'd look at him in amazement and say, "But, darling, that made my knees look fat." He'd look at me, equally bewildered, and reply, "Honey, *fat* was the furthest word from my mind."

In conversations we've had with other couples, all the men, without exception, have said something like, "It is so hard to learn math when someone is sitting next to you wearing a tight sweater." And all of us girls looked at these Neanderthals with disdain for thinking that way.

But apparently boys *do* think that way, no matter how pathetic we women think that is, and it doesn't change when they grow up and get married. Biologically, men feel a need for sex far more frequently than women do. If they don't get release, their bodies will do it for them in their sleep. But even more frequently than they feel the need for sex, they think about sex—one study in Britain reported it's as many as twenty times a day (though other studies say it's as much as every eight seconds!).[6] Indeed, the majority of Christian men still say they suffer from lust, including 38 percent of pastors, according to a *Leadership* magazine survey.[7] It is men's Achilles' heel.

Men are tempted toward lust far more than women because sex is always on parade for them. They see an attractive, curvaceous woman and the first thing they notice is *not* her intelligence. This doesn't mean that they are evil, or sinning, or even that they're sick. They are tempted, which in and of itself is not wrong. As Gene Getz, in the bestseller *The Measure of a Man,* says, "In our culture, men have little control of fleeting thoughts."[8]

We women may have difficulty understanding this temptation because we're not as prone to it. And when our husbands try to explain their struggles, we may ourselves feel temptation: the temptation to hit them over the head with something hard. But we shouldn't react in anger, because that's simply a man's nature. When men are exposed to sexual stimuli day in and day out, sexual tension can build up that is very difficult to deal with. It's similar to how you may feel when you skip a meal: you get really hungry for the next one. When men keep "skipping meals"—building up sexual energy without getting release—they can become almost desperate. They may, to us, appear so pathetic that we wonder, *Who is this sex maniac I married?* But most likely, your husband is not sex crazy. He's just . . . a man.

So here's your first lesson. Repeat this to yourself over and over: "My husband is an alien." He is not made like you. If he desires you frequently, there is nothing wrong with him. Judging him according to your framework isn't fair. He doesn't share it. His desires are not wrong any more than your need for affection is. It's just different. But it's also the way God made him. Obviously he needs to exercise self-control—we all do—but he is not a freak. He is simply a man.

And as a man, he probably saw marriage a little differently than you did. Most Christian men wed rejoicing that now, finally, they can get that release their bodies crave, and they can get it frequently. After all, what's stopping the two of you from having sex as many times as you want to? It's legal now! His liberation has come.

Unfortunately for men—and, it turns out, for women—we don't work the same way. We may dream of making love (we do, after all, have sex drives of our own), but that's not all we need. Men, too, need to feel respected, appreciated, and loved, and not nagged, but good sex can cover a multitude of other problems. Sex is their currency to feel loved.

Society Throws in a Wrench

It's easy to throw up our hands in despair and say, with Kipling, "Ne'er the twain shall meet." Yet no matter how much frustration we have with differing sex drives, at least we're acknowledging the problem exists. The media and the wider society pretend it does not. Popular culture doesn't deal with the difference in sex drives; it portrays women as if we're just like men. When my husband, Keith, was in medical school, professors taught these future doctors that when counseling couples who have sex problems, they should advise the couples to watch pornography together. Pornography, it was thought, would make women excited enough to want to make love. Here's a news flash: women don't work that way. It's not that pornography *can't* make us excited—it can be a big temptation and even an addiction for many—but watching it will not solve the underlying reasons we don't want sex frequently and, as I'll show later, will even make our problems worse. To feel sustained excitement in and commitment to a sexual relationship, we have to feel commitment to the *man*. He comes first, not his hardware.

Our culture does not understand this, as any perusal of magazines or reality shows will testify. I find magazines especially disturbing, since there is virtually no difference in the covers of *Cosmopolitan* (meant for women) and *Maxim* (meant for men). Both men and women are to be lured by the image of a woman—how does one put this politely?—who looks slutty, even though sex-centered lifestyles have horrible repercussions.[9]

Yet the harmful effects aren't limited to those who act out these lifestyles. We, too, internalize some of the messages, including the belief that women should, and do, want sex all the time, too. Before we're married, it's easy to believe it. We have no contrary evidence. When we do marry and find that our sex drives don't require us to act like rabbits twice a day, we're heartbroken. We wonder what's wrong with us. It's not only our husbands who feel cheated; we do, too.

If society treated sex more honestly, this wouldn't be as big a problem. If the women on television weren't as eager to jump into bed as their partners, regardless of what had happened during the day, our husbands might not expect us to act in the same way (and we may not hold that up as our ideal, either). But change in the popular culture is unlikely to happen, so it's time for us to reclaim what is "normal." Normal is not what you see on a magazine cover, or on TV, or in the movies. There may be no such thing as normal. And in a marriage, it doesn't really matter whether Pamela Anderson wants sex all the time, or whether Britney Spears is still a virgin. It doesn't matter how often the average couple makes love or even how often your friends do. All that matters is you and your husband.

Anything you can do to help both you and your husband to stop comparing yourselves to "normal," then, is bound to help your sex life. So here we get to one theme that I will keep coming back to in this book: the biggest enemy of a healthy sex life is in your living room, and I don't mean the dog drooling in your slippers. I mean your TV. It shows unrealistic relationships, tantalizes with beautiful bodies, and helps *you* feel inadequate and *him* tempted, all at the same time! Switch off, and both of you are more likely to "turn on" appropriately.

God Didn't Make a Mistake

Letting go of unrealistic expectations may be liberating, but we're still left with that pesky discrepancy in our sex drives. How could this be the way sex was supposed to be? Yet if you think of the alternative, perhaps it's not so crazy after all. C. S. Lewis says this difference is like "a divine joke; made, I grant you, at our expense, but also [who doubts it?] for our endless benefit."[10] If this benefit isn't immediately apparent, ask yourself this: what would life be like if your husband wasn't interested in sex? Some of you may welcome the temporary reprieve, but in reality, what would happen?

One nice by-product of men wanting sex so much is that they have to be attentive to our needs or risk being rejected. And as they try to butter us up, they also spend time with us. They share our interests and our concerns. They listen to us, and they inevitably become more emotionally attached. Perhaps you're wondering whose husband I'm talking about exactly, since yours has never seemed too interested in this "wooing" business. But most men will consider their wives' feelings to some extent, because that's the only route to what they need.

I'm being a little cynical, since it's in his best interest to be nice to his wife no matter what. After all, everybody is better off if we treat each other with love. Nevertheless, knowing this doesn't stop flare-ups around the world, as any nightly news show will testify. The fact that a man *must* pursue his wife or risk losing one of the most important things to him means that he is more likely to treat her kindly.

At the same time, imagine if we were just as interested in sex as he is. He wouldn't need to treat the relationship well then, either. If sex were purely physical, we would start living out the empty lives spewed across the covers of *Cosmo*—constantly in search of the next greatest pleasure. How easy it would be to drive a wedge between couples! You wouldn't be as interested in *whom* as much as you would be in *what*. With the way God designed it, though, we're creating true intimacy as we meet each other's needs. He becomes more attached to you as he woos you, and you become more devoted to him.

Of course, one could argue that I have just made the case for continuing the status quo. If, for instance, we women all realize that men are desperate for sex, then we can wrap them around our little fingers! Like Herb's wife on *WKRP in Cincinnati*, we could say, "Better mow the grass, Herbie, or no num-nums tonight!" But then two things are going to happen: the intimacy that he hopes to gain from sex is going to evaporate, because as much as he wants and needs it physically, on a spiritual level he wants so much more. He wants a wife who is actively engaged in the process as well, who is eager to show him love by making love instead of just going through the motions. And any attempt at blackmail is going to erode the intimacy that he wants from the act.

But we also jeopardize ourselves. Though we don't need sex to the same extent physically, it still is very beneficial. It releases stress; it builds our immunity; it helps us to feel more intimate; it even increases our lifespan.[11] If we degrade it, we degrade our marriages and ourselves and lose all the positive benefits we derive from a fulfilling sex life.

If we take things one step farther and even give up on sex altogether, what's to distinguish the marriage relationship from any other? We can feel unconditional love for our children; we can be unconditionally supported by our parents; we can live with friends; we can share our problems with counselors. The only thing that is truly unique about marriage is sex.

This uniqueness is something God planned. In 1 Corinthians 7:4–5, Paul writes: "The wife's body does not belong to her alone but also to her husband. In the same way, the husband's body does not belong to him alone but also to his wife. Do not deprive each other except by mutual consent and for a time, so that you may devote yourselves to prayer." This isn't, of course, meant as a sentence of perpetual sexual slavery for women. If your husband's body is yours, then he is not to use his body to take advantage of you, either! But God clearly says the sexual part of your relationship is important and shouldn't be neglected.

I know that may be the last thing you want to hear. I also know that this message has often been distorted. If sin is involved, for instance, I don't believe God wants you to acquiesce to your husband's every sexual demand. Far too many women have allowed their husbands to carry on affairs while still making love to them, hoping that if they don't rock the boat their husbands will come home. Nothing is further from the truth, and if that's where your marriage is, you don't need lingerie; you may need a locksmith! If your sexual problems are this serious, please seek out a Christian counselor or refer to some of the resources listed at the back of this book. But remember, even if you have neglected your husband, you are not to blame for him straying.[12]

Others of you face sin of a different kind. Perhaps he wants to introduce pornography into your sex life, or wants you to do things that you are sure are wrong. In this case, talking to a pastor or a marriage counselor is probably in order.

For most of us, though, it's not adultery or perversion that's worrying us. It's *us*. Maybe you feel taken for granted and tired. Or perhaps you feel flabby. Deep down you wonder whether your husband really finds you attractive, and until you get that reassurance, you can't let go and give yourself to him. Maybe things in your past haunt you. Or perhaps you actually have a great relationship, but you wonder why sex is always such a sore spot. It's the last hurdle you have to cross to make your marriage truly intimate.

Before we move on, let's remember three key things: your husband is an alien, you are not alone, and God made both of you with differing sex drives for a reason. If you understand these three things and can accept by faith that there is a purpose to God's design, then it's time to turn to what that purpose might be.

As we do this, though, I've got to warn you: I'm going to be talking about some difficult attitude shifts we may have to make in order to build truly wonderful and intimate marriages. Of all the chapters in this book, this next one will probably be the hardest, because changing our attitudes about things near and dear to our hearts is always so much harder than changing our wardrobes or our hairstyles. Reading it may even be hazardous to your pillow, if you're the punching type. But give it a chance. Once you get to the end of the book, it will be easier to see how important these attitude changes are and, I pray, easier to let God help you make them.

For Him

Here's your first lesson: Your wife is an alien. She is not like you. Biologically you were made to want sex frequently. She was not. Sex, for a woman, involves letting someone into her body, so it's extremely personal. She has to feel close to you to truly enjoy it, and if your relationship is strained, that's hard. So don't expect her to respond like you do! I've also explained to her how your mind and body work, and told her that you are not abnormal if you want sex frequently.

If you look at magazine covers or people in TV shows, it's easy to believe that women are just like men—that most women salivate for sex at the drop of a hat. Please try not to compare your wife with the women on TV shows. First, they aren't realistic, and, second, you didn't marry them. You married *her*. Honor her, and try to find solutions to this issue that respect her true nature. Remember, she probably wishes she wanted a little more lovin' too, just like you do!

God made you both with differing sex drives for a reason. Your need for sex is primarily physical; hers is primarily relational. If she was as interested in sex as you are, it would diminish your need to care for the emotional aspects of your relationship. As God designed it, if you desire sex, you need to meet her relational needs so that she is willing. It's in your best interest to be nice to her, and as you spend time with her, you'll become more emotionally attached, thereby strengthening your marriage relationship. So there's a purpose to this libido discrepancy!

We're going to turn now to our responsibility for bridging the gap.

Chapter 2

Don't Worry, Be Holy

What is marriage for?

If you heard that question asked in a Sunday school class or on talk radio, you might expect the answer to be to protect kids, to pass on our heritage, or to promote social stability. But if someone had read your mind as you walked down the aisle, chances are they would *not* have heard, "Thank goodness I'm stabilizing society." No, you were getting married because you were in love, and most likely you believed your greatest chance at happiness lay in joining your life with his.

Though we think of marriage in these profoundly personal terms, there's no doubt the first answers would have been correct, too. People who are married are happier and healthier, live longer, and earn more money.[1] (They also have more satisfying sex lives!) They suffer less depression, less substance abuse, and fewer instances of suicide. Children whose parents divorce, on the other hand, are more depressed, do worse in school, and experience more poverty and abuse. Marriage matters.

The reason it matters is that God made us to join together in marriage rather than in casual sexual encounters, and the human species always does better—surprise!—when we follow God's design. We have a vested interest, then, in preserving our marriages, and, if research is to be believed, also a vested interest in improving our sex lives. Susan Heitler found that a great sex life increased people's positive feelings about their marriages by about 15–20 percent. But the results were quite different on the flip side of the equation.

When sexuality is dysfunctional or nonexistent, it plays an inordinately powerful role, from 50–70 percent, draining the marriage of intimacy and good feelings. Paradoxically, bad sex plays a more powerful role in subverting marital satisfaction than good sex does in promoting satisfaction.[2]

If we want to experience all the great benefits marriage has to offer, then we have to seriously consider the state of our sex lives.

Why Marriage?

Ironically, our very reasons for getting married can contribute to our sexual problems. Over the last century, marriage has evolved from something that provided *security* to something that is supposed to provide *fulfillment*. Marriage's potential to provide happiness, though, can be both a luxury and a curse. It's a luxury because we can only think about happiness once our other needs are met. Marriage was once primarily a financial transaction; people tried to marry as well as possible so that their extended family also benefited. When families were hungry, whom you married mattered.

Happiness was a nice by-product, but it wasn't the goal. Even the first romantic poetry written in the early Renaissance was not directed at spouses, but at potential mistresses. Marriage was people's duty, and it wasn't necessarily expected to meet their romantic fantasies. Throughout human history, marriage and even sex were thus devoid of the frantic feelings of love and sexual attraction—or else these feelings came only much later.[3]

Yet today, our society claims that if we don't feel fulfilled, the marriage is meaningless. Watch soap operas and you'll see what I mean. I was once very addicted to *All My Children*. Why was Erica Kane able to marry sixteen different times over twenty years? Because the writers made sure that she never stayed happy. If he doesn't make her happy, you can't expect her to stay! And as you watch, you find yourself rooting for the "other guy," the one who is trying to steal poor Erica away from her current husband. Happiness, you see, is the ultimate good. Yet what pressure this puts on marriages! In such close relationships, we're not always going to feel lovey-dovey.

Besides, by defining happiness this way, we're saying that happiness comes from something others have done, by having others meet our needs for love, affirmation, or even sexual fulfillment. If this is what we believe, we're in for a huge disappointment. Happiness is much more than this. Paul said, "I have learned to be content whatever the circumstances" (Phil. 4:11). How could he be content when he was beaten, in jail, or separated from those he loved? Paul learned that happiness did indeed involve getting our needs met—but it was only the greatest need that counted. And our greatest need is to love God and grow in Him. Ecclesiastes 3:11 tells us that God has "set eternity in the hearts of men." Deep inside everybody is a spiritual yearning, and we can never be happy until that is met. Happiness ultimately depends on God, not on our husbands.

I'm still glad that we have the blessing of marrying for love. When we choose well, and treat marriage well, we are likely to experience a kind of happiness that is perhaps unequalled. But is this really the true purpose of marriage? Happiness is achievable in marriage, just as it is achievable in every area of life if God is our focus—but what if that is not the ultimate goal? As Gary Thomas asks in his book *Sacred Marriage*, what if, instead, marriage was designed to foster *holiness*, to draw us into a more intimate relationship with God?[4] After all, God talks about His relationship to us in marriage terms: He is our bridegroom, and we are the bride. If marriage is primarily about growing closer to God rather than getting our own needs met, this is going to have repercussions on what we do about our sex-drive problem.

What's God Got to Do with It?

Some of you may be reading this thinking, *What has God got to do with it? And how am I supposed to get to the point where I'm not worried about happiness?* I know it sounds strange. You're right; you can't get to that point; not on your own, anyway. But God can change your attitudes from the inside out.

You may know the story about how Jesus died for us. We all have sinned, but God hasn't. In fact, God is so holy that He can't even be around anyone who sins (Isa. 59:2). So if we do things wrong, we can't be with God. But that wasn't good enough for God, because He loved us and wanted us to live with Him. So instead of punishing us for our sins, He made arrangements to come Himself in the form of His Son, and take our penalty by dying so that we can have eternal life with Him.

What a lot of us don't realize is that the story doesn't stop there. We don't just turn from our sins and accept Jesus so that we can go to heaven. Jesus didn't just die; He also rose and lives today. The Bible says He actually comes and lives inside us when we ask Him to. He lives in us so that we can become people who can find happiness, happiness that doesn't come from something outside of us, but true happiness that derives from knowing and loving God, and giving that love away. If you've never found that kind of freedom, I urge you to start reading the Bible and asking God to show Himself to you. If you seek Him, He will come. Find a church you can be a part of, and then you can start to grow in Jesus, finding the freedom and new attitudes that He promises.

Inevitably, as we begin this process of attitude change, it's going to be messy, no matter where we are on our spiritual journey. If our sex difficulties are only about sex, after all, it might be easy enough to sort them out. But if they relate to our attitudes about marriage, and love, and even holiness, then this process gets down and dirty for real: into the worst recesses of ourselves. It's similar to emptying a closet we've ignored for years. I had such a closet in our school room where we homeschool our girls. Everything that did not otherwise have a place in my house was shoved in there. It was scary.

One day I decided to clean it up, and as anyone who has ever undertaken a massive task of this type knows, the first thing you must do is empty everything onto the floor—a task that renders the room a hundred times worse than when you started. You can't stop now, though, because you've just made the whole room unlivable. All the ugly things you'd hoped to forget about are now displayed prominently. But once the stuff is out, it's much easier to deal with. It's the same with these attitude changes we need to make, including our attitudes about what marriage is for.

How Does Marriage Illustrate God's Character?

If you had asked the average woman in the 1990s to name a man who epitomized perfection, many would have said Christopher Reeve. He was well-built, the kind of man who seemed as if he could protect you from anything. He seemed gentle, sophisticated, kind, and faithful to his family.

Yet when he was instantly paralyzed in a horseback riding accident, many wondered what his wife would do. This wasn't just any man; this was Superman. Everything she built her life around came crashing down. Yet Dana Reeve chose to stay. Is she happy? Perhaps that's the wrong question. I imagine she has found that giving herself completely to someone, even when he can't give back in the same way, is very fulfilling.

Most of us aren't asked to give to our husbands like this, but the message is the same: freedom is found in giving. This does not mean that we should allow others to treat us abusively—we are still made in the image of God and are of precious worth to Him. But we can stop asking if *we* are being fulfilled as we start seeking our fulfillment by meeting others' needs. This is how marriage changes us. It works best when we discover the joys of giving.

How Does Marriage Keep Us from Sin?

My friend Rachel grew up in the church and, although she wanted to believe as most of her friends did, she just couldn't. As she grew further from God, she also grew further from her husband, Bill, to whom she'd been unhappily married for seven years. They had a daughter for whom Bill rarely made time, and Rachel was getting sick of it. Finally, the resentment built up and she left the marriage.

Bill hadn't been attentive when they were married, but he loved Rachel. When she left, he was devastated. He started going to bars again, just as he had before they were married. He began picking up women, and his string of one-night stands grew. Bill had never been a believer, but when he was married, even if he was selfish, he was faithful. When Rachel left, he started living a very immoral life. Marriage had kept him, in a way, holy.

But it had also kept Rachel holy. After convincing herself that leaving him wasn't only permissible, but actually good, she started thinking of other decisions not in moral terms but in terms of her own happiness. She moved in with someone who is still, years later, unwilling to commit to her. And Rachel's daughter is watching all of this.

I know many might argue that Rachel shouldn't have to stay in an unhappy marriage, but if you read my book *To Love, Honor, and Vacuum*, I show women like Rachel how they can turn unhappy marriages around, even if their husbands aren't enthusiastic about the process.[5] You don't have to stay unhappy. And even in an unhappy relationship, being married kept Rachel and Bill from sin. It's interesting, but one of the few explicit reasons the Bible actually gives for marriage is to protect us from lust. "It is better to marry than to burn with passion" (1 Cor. 7:9). This in no way says that if your husband has an affair, it's because you weren't meeting his needs. He was the one who chose to sin. But you could play a part in the tempting. If you've ever been on a diet, did you appreciate the friend who urged you to try her chocolate cake because it was "worth the calories"? If you ate it, it was your choice, but it is easier to resist when people support you, isn't it?

So while we are not responsible for a husband's choice to sin, think of the privilege we have in helping to relieve some temptation! We, in essence, can contribute to their holiness. I know that's hardly an aphrodisiac, and you're probably not leaping out of your chair with rapturous cheers. Yet think about it: if God gave us the opportunity to help our kids steer clear of sin, we would jump at it in an instant. Somehow we think husbands, though, should be able to fend for themselves. We love our husbands, so let's humble ourselves to accept this challenge. We don't just need to make our sex life better to stop him from sulking; we can also preserve the relationship that God ordains, help keep our husbands holy, and even encourage greater holiness in ourselves.

Creating Holy Marriages

Making a wholehearted commitment to creating this kind of marriage is the first step in changing your sex life. That's because sex can only be fulfilling on every level when commitment is part of it. A piece of paper cannot guarantee that commitment. Many of us are in our marriages conditionally—*I'll see how things go in the next few years, but I can't live like this forever.*

I met Jennifer, thirty-eight, at a retreat. She's in the middle of a testing time in her marriage. When she married her husband ten years ago, she knew he wasn't the love of her life. He did want her, though, and he was the first one ever to do so. She forgot to ask herself, "Do I like him?" because she was too busy reveling in the fact that somebody finally liked her! Ten years later she feels miserable. Her husband rarely lifts a finger around the house and never takes an interest in her, and she feels very alone.

So many women are like Jennifer. Many of us marry people who don't treat us well simply because that's what we're used to. By the time we recognize this dynamic, it's too late to change. When you're in a marriage like this, staying hardly seems fair. Yet even if you would have done differently if you had to do it over again, it won't help you to daydream about all the "what ifs." Studies show that your best chance of finding peace and contentment is in your marriage, even if such a thing sounds impossible.[6]

Commitment can sometimes sound like a dirty word, as if it's something that holds us down. Like the tethers on a hot air balloon, it stops us from experiencing all life has to offer. And yet nothing is further from the truth. Until you commit to a relationship, you can't discuss problems. If you do discuss them, the other may leave. So the relationship is a shallow one. Commitment allows a relationship to grow deep and happiness to bloom.

Commit to Change

Commitment to the marriage isn't all we need; we also need commitment to making the marriage work, and this means taking the initiative, even if our husbands aren't acknowledging their problems. This isn't something God asks of you that He has never done Himself. Paul said, "While we were yet sinners, Christ died for us" (Rom. 5:8). Even when we were doing things that broke His heart, Jesus gave Himself for us. And now He says, "Your attitude should be the same" (Phil. 2:5).

This is awfully difficult, especially if we're hurt. Chances are, though, that when we do feel hurt we focus on whether he's fulfilling our needs, rather than on whether we're fulfilling his. Acknowledging our needs is important, and I don't mean to minimize it. But, as we've seen, our greatest need is actually to grow closer to God. In the Sermon on the Mount, Jesus says,

> Why do you look at the speck of sawdust in your brother's eye and pay no attention to the plank in your own eye? How can you say to your brother, "Let me take the speck out of your eye," when all the time there is a plank in your own eye? You hypocrite, first take the plank out of your own eye, and then you will see clearly to remove the speck from your brother's eye. (Matt. 7:3–5)

Let's focus on the things that *we're* doing wrong, rather than on what he's doing that bothers us. Interestingly, Jesus doesn't say we're to ignore our husband's sin in perpetuity; only that we can't help him until we deal with our own problems. Work on fulfilling his needs—living up to your part of the bargain—and the rest will fall into place. You don't have to figure out *how* you're going to do that yet. Just know that focusing on him first, radical as it sounds, can actually make you far less frustrated in the long run.

Give Up Your Need to Be Right

Committing to change means letting go of your need to be right. This isn't something we find easy. Women tend to want to be seen as the "good ones" in the marriage. We usually feel far more vulnerable in relationships than men do, something that Mary Stewart VanLeeuwen attributes to the curse of the Fall.[7] If we admit to being wrong, we give our husbands a reason to leave. So instead we have to prove that *they* are the ones who need to improve so they understand what a good deal they've got. Why would someone with as many faults as he has leave a relationship? Who else is going to take someone so messed up? We have a vested interest in preserving the status quo, where he is seen as the one who is too demanding, too insensitive, and too unromantic.

Yet if you were able to cast aside this need to be validated and concentrate on him, you may be pleasantly surprised. Jesus says, "Whoever wants to save his life will lose it, but whoever loses his life for me will find it" (Matt. 16:25). In that passage, Jesus is talking about letting go of the things on this earth that matter most to us. As we do, we'll find our happiness, our fulfillment, and our peace. That's exactly the holiness, and eventually the happiness, that marriage can inspire.

I am *not* saying that you should be your husband's slave (see my book *To Love, Honor, and Vacuum* for more about this), nor am I saying that you should give up your right to be respected. Feeling respected is an important part of a healthy, intimate sexual relationship, as we will see soon. What I *am* saying is that the more you cling to your own need to be right, the more you put up a roadblock to productive change in your marriage.

Forgive Him

Sometimes this requires forgiving him for very real sins against you. Perhaps he had an affair years ago that he has asked forgiveness for and tried to make right. You accepted him back, but at some level you're still punishing him. Or maybe you had major sexual difficulties because of abuse in your past, and instead of being supportive and understanding, he was selfish. Harboring bitterness, though, only hurts you.

Jesus put no limits on forgiveness. Philip Yancey, in his book *What's So Amazing About Grace?* admits that forgiveness is an "unnatural act."[8] Extending grace to someone who does not deserve it feels just plain wrong. Yet just as Jesus already paid for the guilt you feel, He already paid for your husband's guilt, too. Best of all, forgiveness has a side effect that nothing else can deliver: it brings a marvelous freedom to both of you. Your husband is set free to love you, unencumbered by the need to "make amends," and you are free from the cycle of "ungrace" that demands a retribution that can never be paid.

Unforgiveness is probably the biggest barrier to healing. It takes such humility and strength to say, "I will no longer hold this against you," and often we just don't feel up to the task. As hard as it seems to forgive, though, it is so much harder to live with bitterness. You may be protecting your need to be right, but you give up your only chance at freedom and peace, and you limit what God can do in your family.

There is, unfortunately, a caveat to this advice. If the sin that needs forgiving is something that endangers your marriage or your children, such as abuse or infidelity, then forgiveness, while necessary, is not the only step you need to take. If he's abusing you or your children, get out. There isn't an excuse for hurting you, and you need to save yourself, even if forgiveness may, indeed, be part of the spiritual way in which you do this later on.

Let Go of the Tug of War over Sex

Sex can easily degenerate into a tug of war, with both spouses feeling rejected and punishing each other for it. Men feel as if their wives don't really love them, and women feel used. For some wives, the more her husband ignores her feelings and pressures her to have sex, the more she starts to equate sex with something that hurts her. To feel loved, what she really wants is for him to not want it at all.

However, if you can make a decision now to think of sex as a gift you can give to him—a gift you can have just as much fun unwrapping as he can—its capacity to hurt you is gone. If you can take the initiative, you don't need to worry about whether he's considering your feelings.

Before you get ready to throw this book against the wall and swear that such a thing is impossible, hear me out. When I was first married, I took a book that urged compromise in this area and "drowned" it—sticking it underwater in the bathtub until I was sure it was dead and then dumping it unceremoniously in the garbage. The authors obviously didn't understand how I felt.

I do understand how difficult this area of your life can be, particularly because sex is such a profoundly personal thing. I don't expect you to say, "Well, I'm just going to forget the past and everything's going to be better now," and slither into bed beside him. What I hope to do is to give you a blueprint so that such things may, in the end, be possible.

Even if you don't know how this will work physically or practically because of other problems, you can still change your attitudes and your goals. Get your mind in line, and then we'll work on the rest. And if you start to be generous, you'll feel relief because you're not keeping score. And your husband? He'll feel gratitude, intimacy, and satisfaction. He'll likely treat you better than he's done lately, so you'll feel happier, too. It's a win-win for everyone.

And, on a lighter note, you'll probably get much more sleep! Remember Andrea, who knew that if she followed her husband Jeff out of the bedroom, they'd just argue for hours? One nurse gave a patient in a similar situation this advice: "Every time he asks you and you're not driving down the highway, say *yes!* Take ten minutes; you'll spend longer than that arguing about it."[9] From experience, I think she has a point!

For Him

Lest you despair that your marriage is never going to get better, let me tell you why you should be happy that you're married! You're likely to live longer, make more money, be happier, be healthier, and have a better sex life (believe it or not) than your playboy friends. Marriage matters, because that's how God made us.

Yet our reasons for marriage, ironically, can often undermine our relationships. Did you get married because you thought it would make you happy? Because you thought your wife could meet your needs? If you did, you're probably pretty miserable right now. So try this on for size: what if marriage is not for happiness, but instead for holiness? What if marriage can make us happy ultimately, but God really instituted it to bring us closer to Him? It's easy to see how this can work. Holiness has two sides. The first, and the one that most readily comes to mind, is absence of sin. But there's also the flipside: holiness is acting as Jesus did, considering others first and giving to them. Marriage encourages us to do both of these things. In fact, our marriage relationships work best when we give to each other, but they also keep all of us, and especially men, from the sin of lust.

If that's the case, think about this question over the next few days: How can I act in a more holy way toward my wife? How can I make sure my body is truly hers, instead of making demands on her with it? (I've encouraged her to consider giving to you in this way, as well, don't worry!)

Let me give you a couple of hints: when you come home from work, or when you leave in the morning, kiss her without any expectation of anything sexual. Take her out for dinner, go home, enjoy some leisurely kisses, and then roll over and go to sleep. It may sound radical, but you're showing her that you're willing to meet her needs for affection, even if she doesn't meet yours. It's like you're making a deposit in her bank account, and the higher your balance is, the easier it will be to make withdrawals later.

Take a deep breath, say a prayer, and see if you can do it, even if it's just for a time.

Chapter 3

Heads, Shoulders, Knees, and Toes

Advertising is filled with some absolutely ridiculous promises. This face cream will erase the fact that you have four kids, two dogs, and a job. This toilet bowl cleaner will make you so happy you'll leap for joy. Little is more ridiculous than the e-mail promises whereby men can grow various parts of their anatomy by several inches and grow hair on others (at least we hope it's others). But one recent promise actually sounded plausible: Technology was going to save us time. We could relax in our hammocks while computers planned our perfectly balanced nutritional meals, ovens automatically cooked our dinners, and air purifiers did our dusting.

What a letdown. The only thing that air purifier in my bedroom is doing is giving me one more disgusting thing I have to clean out every two months. And my computer isn't busy planning my menus; it's eating up my time as I become addicted to e-mail!

Technology has not freed us. We work harder than ever, we have less free time than before, and we're always tired. So far, we've looked at the attitude changes we need to make to help our sex lives. Now let's turn to this exhaustion problem, since it's one of the easiest libido destructors to diagnose and treat. Relationship changes and self-image issues are also important in this quest for sexual happiness, but they're harder, and I like doing the most straightforward things first.

Often we get so busy that it feels like there's no way to fit sex into our schedules. But if we're honest, time really isn't the issue. Virtually all of us have the *time* to have sex. For most of us, it doesn't necessarily even take that long. There may be nights when we do want it to last longer, but on the whole we tend to be content with sexual encounters that are long enough to feel good, but not so long that we start to worry that the kids should be waking up for school sometime soon.

Our problem, instead, is that we don't have the *energy*. A survey done by Mead Johnson in 2000 found that 80 percent of women reported feeling more tired now than they had five years ago, and 83 percent of them reported feeling "tired and weak" as their number one health complaint.[1] Finding that magical formula to rev our batteries is our greatest challenge. I've tried drinking several Diet Pepsi's a day for almost a year now (I hate coffee), and I would not recommend it. We cannot manufacture energy.

Our challenge with energy is similar to the challenge of harnessing solar power. Theoretically, solar power should be the cheapest and easiest form of energy, but it hasn't taken off because it's hard to store. You may have a ton of power at noon, but how do you build a battery large enough to keep it until nighttime? Humans are the same way. We have energy at some points during the day, but not necessarily when we most want it. Even worse, we also drain our battery on unnecessary things so it's empty before we really need it. If we're going to feel more energetic, we need to capture energy, save it, and store it. Let's look at how all that is possible.

Charging Our Batteries

Sleep

The surest way to capture energy is to sleep. Ironically, despite how far we've "progressed" in the last century, we seem to have forgotten this. If you read books from 150 years ago, you'll find that most people went to sleep with the sun. They slept about ten hours a night, which was why it was easier for them to get up at dawn to milk the cows.[2] Why did they sleep? One reason was that they couldn't see at night. Candles were expensive, and there was no electricity, so sleep was the natural thing to do.

But it's no longer as natural, thanks to Thomas Edison. Bright lights trick our brains into thinking it's time to be productive when it's not. And now, because it's easy to stay up late and still get things done, it has become almost a status symbol to see how little sleep we need to function.

James Maas, author of *Power Sleep,* thinks we're heading for trouble. The vast majority of us are suffering from a sleep deficit that can have profound consequences. If we don't get the sleep we need, we become grumpy and irritable, and we lose concentration. On the health side, we become more prone to depression, viral illnesses, and all kinds of other problems. Lack of sleep is also implicated in more than 100,000 traffic accidents a year, making it the leading killer on the road.[3]

Getting enough sleep on a regular basis can be revolutionary. Our outlook on life can completely change. Our problems are minimized, and some may even disappear. But often we overlook how important sleep actually is. Jimmy Carter and Bill Clinton were both presidents who believed their job was too important to sleep.[4] George W. Bush thinks the exact opposite, and he turns in by 10:00. He knows it's the only way he can handle the responsibility of his job.[5] If he can make time for sleep, surely we can, too. Here are some tips for catching some *Zs.*

Training Your Body to Sleep

Do you have trouble falling asleep? Sometimes it may be because you're worried, but often there is a far simpler cause. Perhaps you haven't trained your body when to sleep, and it's confused. You may fall into bed at 9:00 one night, absolutely exhausted, but then on the weekend stay up until 1:30 in the morning because you want some fun for a change. After a while, your body doesn't know when it's bedtime.

If you want to help your body to sleep (those with healthy sleep patterns drift off in less than ten minutes), then go to sleep at the same time every night and get up at the same time every day. Even on weekends. Even when school's done. Even on holidays. Get into a routine, and your body will thank you.

You may take my advice and find out how great this works. Or you may be wishing I was in the room with you right now so that you could say, "But you don't know my kids!" or even, "You try sleeping next to my husband when he's snoring." So let's look at some of the other impediments to getting proper rest, turning first to the smallest and most disturbing.

Helping Infants Learn to Sleep

Babies are physically capable of sleeping through the night around three months of age. Once they're able to do without their midnight feeding, lessons in sleeping can begin.

Teaching a child to sleep sounds strange, but it is absolutely necessary. At one point, our home life looked something like this: to get our little Katie to sleep, she needed to be nursed in a rocking chair. Then, when it looked like she was in a deep sleep, she had to be lifted without any change in the angle of her body, even if this required me putting my back seriously out. Then, I had to frantically call, "Keith, Keith, get in here!" in order to summon my husband to rearrange the blankets and lower the crib rail (since I usually forgot to do this before I started nursing). Everything thus readied, I could effect the perfect transfer without changing the angle of Katie's body.

If any of these conditions were not met—and, in many cases, even if they were—Katie would cry. In this case, what she needed was to be transferred to the swing. Once she was again in a deep sleep, one of us could pick her up and attempt the transfer once again. This was much more dangerous, because it necessitated changing the angle of her body, which usually woke her up, sending us back to step one (nurse her in a rocking chair). Because this was our nightly ritual—and our middle-of-the-night ritual—Katie could get to sleep no other way.

One day we smartened up. We read Richard Ferber's book *Solve Your Child's Sleep Problems,* which said that babies need to be taught how to go to sleep by themselves.[6] They need to be put in their cribs awake, both at set nap times and set bedtimes, so they get used to putting themselves to sleep.[7] Otherwise, you're teaching your baby to need you to sleep, and whenever that baby wakes in the night, he or she will call for you. Reading this was like that revelation at the end of *Planet of the Apes*, when the main character looks at the desolation on the earth, and collapses in grief as he realizes, "We did this to ourselves!"

Amazingly, within three days, Katie had learned to sleep. And she started taking naps, too, once we made them at regular times. And once she started to sleep, she started to smile. And finally so did I.

"Can I Sleep with You?"

My happy story with Katie ended once she moved out of the crib and into her own bed. Now she could get out of her bed and crawl into mine. She's a snuggler, something for which, for about sixteen hours of the day, I'm very grateful. But it's just not as attractive a characteristic at 2:30 in the morning. Kids kick, and I had enough of that when I was pregnant. But it's not just the kicking. Katie's idea of snuggling with Mommy is to throw her arms tightly around my neck, line up our noses, and wrap her legs around me. As much surface area as possible must touch Mommy at all times, and then she can sleep.

I don't sleep well when my children are in the bed, and studies show that I'm not alone. Yet sleeping separately from Mommy and Daddy is important for another reason, too: children must, from the very beginning, realize that Mommy and Daddy have a relationship apart from them, one that will go on when children leave. Kids can climb in to snuggle and read bedtime stories, but this is Mommy and Daddy's bed. That's important not only for the kids to know, but for you to know, too. If the bed is reserved for your own relationship, even the part that's not necessarily sexual, it will be easier to nurture that sexual part.

Nevertheless, this doesn't answer the question of what to do when Katie tries to climb in at 2:30 in the morning. I always felt a little guilty not allowing her into my bed after she'd had a nightmare until we watched a wonderful movie called *Ruby Bridges*. In it, the little girl, who is the first African-American child to be integrated into a white school, has a nightmare and wants her mother. Her mother asks firmly but kindly, "Have you prayed to Jesus yet?" She shakes her head no, and her mother marches her back to her bedroom. "You go to Jesus first," she says gently. Once our children are old enough to do this (and we may have to do it with them for a while), what a wonderful gift we can give to show them that they don't need us to go to God!

Why Aren't They Home Yet?

Unfortunately, the sleep problems kids cause don't end once they're potty trained and can deal with nightmares. When children are teenagers, they can give you the nightmares instead. They venture out, and you can't sleep until they return home to the nest.

Ensuring that your children treat you with respect, though, can help to alleviate some of these fears. Have a reasonable curfew, and make sure they stick to it. If they don't, give them some stern and immediate consequences, because they have worried you unnecessarily. Don't let them go out the next weekend, or don't let them use the phone for a time. Let them know you're serious.

You can also start the phone rule: They must call you when they arrive to tell you where they are, and they must call if they're going to be late. Letting teens have a cell phone can also calm your fears if you can call them and find out where they are.

Finally, make sure that your children know that your main concern is their safety. If they're in an uncomfortable situation, let them know they can always call you to go get them without incurring your wrath. If you know they'll take this step, then it's less likely that you will have to lie at home wondering what they could be up to.

Sleeping Next to a Buzz Saw

Janet's husband goes to sleep as soon as his head hits the pillow. Janet is almost into dreamland herself when the bed starts vibrating as if being sawn to pieces. Her chance of sleep is once more gone. She considers shaking him awake and making him turn over, but that never solves the problem for more than a few minutes. Resigned, she grabs the top blanket from the bed (pulling it out from under him a little bit roughly), takes her pillow, and marches off for one more night on the narrow couch.

When we marry, we dream of contentedly drifting off in each other's arms. But that's before we realize we're married to Thomas the Tank Engine. And a depressing 1999 study found that the spouse of a snorer will never really get used to this. Studying couples in which one partner was a chronic snorer, Dr. John Shepard, Medical Director of the 1999 Mayo Clinic Sleep Disorders Study, reports that when a spouse snores, the non-snoring spouse wakes up on average twenty times per hour, even if only briefly. In total, the non-snorers lost an average of one hour of sleep per night, leading Dr. Shepard to suggest that partners of chronic snorers suffer from a sleep disorder themselves.[8]

People snore more if they eat a lot before coming to bed, gain weight, drink alcohol, or have a cold. Sometimes tilting the head of the bed up can help. A pair of earplugs got me through university with three roommates. (In truth they weren't that noisy, I was just an incredibly light sleeper.) If none of these solutions work, you may have to consider sleeping apart. Many of us balk at this idea because we're scared of sacrificing the intimacy of sharing a bed. It's often while lying together that we have our most important conversations and hash out our differences.

But if you put your mind to it, you can preserve these moments and still protect your sleep. Try retiring together, in bed, a little earlier than you usually go to sleep. Use that time to do something together, such as sharing a psalm. Then take some time to talk about your day, to pray, and even to have sex.

After you've spent some time together, separate before actually going to sleep. Make up a comfortable guest bed, or tuck a pillow and blankets into a basket by the couch, so that no one has to struggle in the middle of the night to put a bed together. To avoid any lingering resentment if you don't have a guest room, take turns being the one to leave the bed, so that both spouses get to enjoy the bedroom. And be sure to tell your children and others who need to know about the sleeping arrangements, so they won't assume your marriage is on the rocks!

Finally, keep the process devoid of blame. My grandfather married a horrific snorer, but he was deaf without his hearing aids in, so it made no difference to him. Snoring is not the problem in itself; the combination of snorer and light sleeper is. It's not time to lay blame; it's just time to get some sleep!

Building a Bigger Battery

Sleep is not the only thing that creates our energy. Spending our energy also creates the capacity for more. If you have a portable phone that runs on a traditional battery, you know what I mean. Leave it on the cradle, and the battery soon won't last very long. Let the phone run dead before you recharge it, though, and it will keep its large capacity. You have to spend energy to create endurance. Exercise works the same way. My mother recently lost about fifty pounds by committing herself to exercise. One of the benefits she has found is that she's far less tired than she was before she started all this huffing and puffing.

Nevertheless, few of us can get excited by a treadmill. I have an elliptical machine that is a wonderful dust collector in my bedroom (it feeds that air purifier). One of these days I'm going to just accept the fact that I'm not a workout kind of person and get rid of the thing, but right now I'm still holding on to illusions of myself.

Yet even though I can't use an elliptical machine, I can still exercise. I find exercise works better for me when it's a social activity. Katie likes doing aerobics with me, so we often put on a fast CD and jump around together. We also take bike rides and walks together. (When my kids were smaller I pulled them in a bike trailer.) My friend Michelle, a youth worker and mother of three, also believes exercise is easier if you can combine it with building relationships. She invited a neighbor to walk with her several times a week in the early morning, and a new friendship was born.

You can also nurture your marriage in a similar way by doing something you both enjoy, like ballroom dancing, swimming, or walking. Do something active, and your body will be more energetic for other things in your life (you'll sleep better, too!).

Energy has another important side effect: it increases our sex drives and makes it easier for us to experience sexual pleasure. Building muscle tone and endurance helps us "keep up" with sex, but cardio workouts also increase blood flow everywhere, making it easier to become, and stay, aroused. In fact, Cindy Meston from the University of Texas found that exercise was a key factor in sexual response. "It wasn't that the exercise itself was making the women in the study sexually aroused," says Meston. "Rather, exercise prepared the body in some way for [sex]."[9] Meston explains that for men, sexual dysfunction tends to be a function of anxiety, so remedies usually focus on relaxation. For women, the physiology appears different. It turns out we respond better when our hearts are pumping!

Perhaps the best time to work out, then, may be in the early evening. More research from New Mexico suggests that this may be just the recipe we need to rev our sex drives. Testosterone levels peak for women after a workout.[10] Though some studies have shown that exercise tends to wake us up, making it harder to get to sleep, studies also show that a satisfying sexual encounter will make us tired. Hopefully, then, the latter will compensate for the former, so we can still sleep even after exercising both in the bed and out!

Filling Up with Energy

The last way we can get energy is actually the most direct: we eat it. Yet what we eat and when we eat can affect our energy levels for better or for worse. Cutting down on carbohydrates at lunchtime, for instance, can help us to overcome that need for a 2:00 nap.

When I eat macaroni and cheese for lunch, I have to drag myself through the afternoon. But if I eat a chicken salad, with lots of protein and green vegetables, I'm much more energetic! Most of us lose steam in the middle of the afternoon, and then, when evening comes, it's easy to feel like we let the day get away from us. These small changes to your diet can keep you alert, helping you to get more done so that you can end the day satisfied. If you feel that way before you turn off the light, chances are greater that you'll feel that way afterwards, too.

Preserving That Battery

Now that our batteries have stored more energy, we have to make sure we don't spend it on the wrong things. And that means we must get out the weed whacker and cut, cut, cut. Get rid of all the things in your life that drain you.

Clutter

Look around your bedroom. Are the surfaces clear, or are they piled with clutter? Is laundry waiting to be folded? Are bills waiting to be paid? All of that stuff causes stress. Most of us have clutter because it's easier to hang on to stuff than to throw it away. Yet clutter brings difficulties of its own. It's much easier to keep kids' drawers neat, for instance, if they only have eight or nine changes of clothes rather than twenty. And it's easier to find a nice pair of earrings if your jewelry box isn't filled with junk.

If you're having trouble getting rid of clutter, here's what Marla Cilley, otherwise known as Flylady from www.flylady.net, recommends. Go through your house room-by-room armed with three different boxes. Look critically at everything that's there. Have you used it in the last year? Fill one box for the dump, one for charity, and one for things you're not sure you're ready to give up. Then put the last one away, tape it, and label it with the date a year from today. If, on that date, you haven't had a need to go into the box, then give it to charity without opening it. You didn't need it anyway.

Commitments

Stuff is not the only thing we need to throw out; we also need to get rid of things that directly eat up time. Recently my husband and I quit several committees. It wasn't because we didn't think they were worthwhile causes; it was because we didn't have time to play Monopoly with our kids.

It's all too easy to become so busy that we have no time to relax at home. And that relaxing time is important for keeping tabs on our relationships with both our spouses and our kids. There are days when I feel that the only thing coming out of my mouth is "Hurry up, girls! We've got to go!" I've found that the only way to stop hurrying is to have nowhere to go.

You may feel guilty about giving up things at church because that's "ministry"; that's what we *should* be doing. But I'm not sure that our primary ministry needs to be inside the church doors. Look at Jesus. He didn't go around inviting people to the temple. He went to their parties instead. He got to know people where they were most comfortable. And our primary ministry should not be to feed those who are already in the fold as much as it is to bring new people there. But we won't have time to build friendships in a low stress environment if we're perpetually busy.

Sometimes it's not *our* commitments that make us hurry; it's our kids'. Many of our children are overinvolved in after-school activities (or even preschool activities), to the point that we feel more like chauffeurs than parents. Kids do not need to be involved in everything under the sun. Chances are that you were not, but the norm today is for kids to be enrolled in everything possible.

Part of this is to keep them busy while both parents are at work. But part is also a reaction to the dangers we now perceive in our community. Kids thirty years ago would have been free to go to the park and throw the ball around on a Saturday morning. Now we have to enroll them in soccer, because we don't let our kids wander to the park anymore. Everything has to be supervised, planned, and organized, and it takes a lot more work on our part. Teenagers, too, may need to be driven to part-time jobs, further eating into our time.

If your children are getting too involved, sit down with them and talk about limiting their activities. Let them choose one or two activities, and save the rest for a one-week summer camp. If your teens are running your life ragged, see if they can get a job that's closer or that's on a bus route so that driving doesn't take up too much of your time.

Giving up extra activities gives us the freedom to say "yes" to other things that are not constant commitments. It allows us to have those neighbors that we have such fun with over for coffee. It gives us the flexibility to rent a movie and pop some popcorn and snuggle together as a family. And that's the sort of thing that will lift your spirits and feed your soul.

People Who Sap Your Energy

It's 2:30 in the afternoon, you need to leave for your part-time job in fifteen minutes, and you're madly putting in one last load of laundry and sticking the meatloaf in the oven for your husband before you have to go.

In the middle of the chaos the phone rings. It's your sister Sharon. She left her husband last year and has been involved with another man who seems unwilling to make a commitment. She is very depressed, and often talks about how maybe she should just cash everything in. You are her lifeline, she says. You always listen so well. So she launches into another discussion about how Jim, her ex-husband whom you always liked, wants to divvy up the house and is upset because she hasn't yet called a realtor, but he doesn't understand how hard it is for her because she's so depressed. And Derek, the new boyfriend, hasn't called in more than two days, and last time he was here he just wanted to watch the game and totally ignored her, and now what is she to do?

You begin to panic. The clock is ticking, the laundry is spinning, but your sister hasn't paused for a breath yet. She hasn't called to talk with you; she's called to talk *at* you. She never asks about the kids, never asks how you're doing, and never asks if this is a good time.

Many of us have Sharons in our lives. They sap all of our energy, almost like they're black holes. They say things to try to make us feel guilty if we try to escape, and our day is ruined after speaking with them. We're annoyed, but at the same time we're worried because we really do care.

Other friends may not be draining in the same way, but they still leave us in a funk. My friend Susan recently had her second baby. Mickaula, her first, was perfect. She slept through the night early. She fed on schedule. She rarely fussed. Then came Blake. Blake was not content to sit happily watching Susan vacuum. He wanted to be played with, to be picked up, or simply to cry.

Some of Susan's friends also had babies, and their babies more closely resembled Mickaula than they did Blake. These friends offered all kinds of advice on how to cope, showing Susan how everything she was doing was completely wrong. Susan was soon a nervous wreck. She was exhausted, and now she felt guilty, too.

What Susan needed was to drown out all those other voices. Certainly there are times when we could use some good advice. But often what would really help is if people just left us alone, or at least stopped drawing attention to how well they cope with these same problems.

If you are surrounded by friends like Susan's, perhaps it's time to find a new circle of friends, even if it's just temporarily. Let God tell you whether what you are doing is best or not, and seek His opinion by reading Scripture, being quiet before Him, reading books that speak to your heart, and seeking godly mentors. If a friend's advice isn't in line with what God is telling you, then you need to stay away and learn to silence the condemnation.

Back to black-hole Sharon. Banishing her, especially if she is a relative, is much trickier. Try beginning the conversation by setting some boundaries. Say, "Sharon, I have five minutes to talk, and then I have to go." If she doesn't listen, hang up. It is not loving to allow someone to use you; it is encouraging the person to be selfish. If you struggle in this area, read Henry Cloud and John Townsend's book *Boundaries*,[11] and pray for God to help you limit people. Remember that even Jesus took time away from crowds to connect with the Father. You need—and deserve—time by yourself.

Banish Chaos

If you've eliminated unwanted telephone calls and quit several committees, chances are the word *hurry* won't be coming out of your mouth as frequently as it once did. But chaos can also infect our homes themselves.

A house that runs smoothly requires organization. We need to know what has to be done, plan it, and—here's the hard part—do it! If you work outside the home during the day, it's hard to get the energy to run the house. But even stay-at-home moms can find themselves living in chaos. The reason? We don't organize our time. If we did, no matter what our work situations are, we'd likely find that housework actually took far less time than it does now.

I spent a large chunk of my book *To Love, Honor, and Vacuum* helping women organize their homes so they could free up time for relationships. I can't deal with everything here, but let me touch on the main issues. First, let's treat the house like it's our job. At an important job, you work hard to get everything done as quickly and efficiently as possible. You don't procrastinate by reading e-mails, reading the paper, or talking on the phone (or maybe you do, but it's still not a good idea!). When I let the computer get the better of me, it's not hard for a whole hour or two to go by with me having nothing to show for it. The rest of the day I have to play catch-up, and my children pick up on my stress, making everything worse.

To keep myself on track, I find it helpful to plan my day the night before. Every evening I look at tomorrow's day: what appointments or activities we have, what I'm making for lunch and dinner, what errands I need to run, and what part of the house I'm going to clean (I never tackle everything at once). Then, as I sleep, this schedule solidifies in my mind.

Planning our menu and our grocery list can also be tremendously helpful in reducing our stress level. Leanne Ely, author of *Saving Dinner*, believes dinner "is a place of communion and fellowship, and a means of reconnecting with those we care about the most. Over a simple family meal, important stuff happens."[12] When we don't plan, though, dinners become haphazard, or even worse, get off to a bad start when we have to drag cranky kids to the grocery store several times a week to get something at the last minute. Planning eliminates chaos, whining, worry, and most grocery trips, and lets us build relationships in peace over dinner.

When it comes to cleaning, an organizational plan can also transform your home. I concentrate on only one room a day, but I'm constantly clearing away clutter. Every day at 4:00, for half an hour before I start to make dinner, I go through all the rooms and get rid of the clutter that's built up over the day. Because the surfaces stay clean, it takes very little effort to dust (my kids do this). Once a week I vacuum and mop. But I never feel like I have to clean the whole house on any one day because I stay on top of the mess.

Anyone who comes into my house might be surprised when they read this, because I make it sound like I'm very neat, but I'm not. I don't aim for perfection; I aim for clutter-free, so that I can have friends over without being embarrassed. To me, that's all that's important: keeping a comfortable, but not a perfect, house.

If you start treating your domestic life with the kind of organization that you would give to a job, you'll find everything in your home goes a lot more smoothly. Cleaning won't take as much time, because things won't get as dirty. You won't waste as much time running to the store, because you won't be left at the last minute without necessary ingredients. And you won't feel the stress that comes from a messy house. All of these things can give us more energy, because we're not wasting energy on counterproductive things.

You're well-rested. You're energetic. Now, when the evening comes, you can relax! You've organized your life so there's no need to panic. For some, the idea of lying in his arms and making both of you feel great is now a lot more doable—and appealing! Others of us have more steps we need to take before sex becomes less stressful. Let's turn next to some of the harmful ideas we may have about sex that get in the way of a fulfilling marriage

For Him

Men seem to be able to handle being tired better than women do. For relationship sparks, though, she first has to have enough sleep. Encourage her to go to bed at the same time every night and to get up at the same time every morning—to train her body to sleep at the right time and to give her energy when she needs it. If you can, go to bed with her and get up with her, too.

Treat snoring seriously. If you snore, she could be chronically exhausted. Try losing weight; don't have a beer within a few hours of going to bed; and don't overeat at dinner. If that doesn't work, try sleeping with the head of the bed slightly tilted up. Finally, if she still can't sleep, take turns sleeping in separate rooms, after spending some time together first.

Help her get rid of the things in her life that sap her energy. If your house is cluttered, then her life is stressful. Are your trophies everywhere? Do you have papers all over the bedroom? This adds a kind of mental stress that you may not share. Let go of some of your old stuff and let her sort out the house! She'll feel a lot better.

Banish chaos. Help her to figure out what commitments she and the kids can get out of to save time. If your relatives or friends also make her life chaotic, support her in needing her space. Toxic people can make her feel guilty and exhausted for hours afterward. Help her get away from them—even if it's your mother—and she's more likely to relax later at night with you!

Chapter 4

Throw Out That Bath Water

I know a lot about the sex life of lizards. It's not something I'm particularly proud of or even something I'm particularly happy about. But my husband is allergic to all animals with hair, so it was inevitable.

You see, my older daughter, Rebecca, loves animals. When she turned seven, she naturally decided she wanted a pet. She had to choose between getting a fluffy puppy and keeping Daddy, and she wisely settled for her father. In return, we agreed to purchase one of the few pets that lacks hair follicles: a leopard gecko.

Now Spotty, our lizard, is kind of cute. He kind of grows on you, even with that eating-live-crickets habit. So when Spotty had his first birthday, my children decided it was time to try to mate him. They wanted some little Spottys. My husband agreed, and so somehow I ended up being a fertility consultant for reptiles. It's enough to make one think democracy is highly overrated.

We dutifully borrowed a female leopard gecko from a friend and put the two together. There was only one problem. Either our lizard is gay or he's extremely stupid. He didn't seem to do anything except try to hide from her. We consulted with a gecko specialist, and he suggested that we put a few more males in the tank to give Spotty a feeling of competition. When he felt threatened, the logic went, he would perform.

This wasn't exactly the lesson on reproduction we wanted to teach our daughters, so we simply told them that Spotty wasn't in love and let it go at that. Yet during this whole sordid episode in my family's life, it occurred to me that, in many ways, our society tries to treat humans as if we are lizards: you see a mate, and you procreate. We treat sex as if it's something purely instinctive, not something imbued with all the relational and emotional components that God gave it.

Respecting Our Fragile Sexuality

The relational components of sex are what make it so special. Consider this: humans are the only creatures that can mate face to face. Sex isn't only about our bodies. Because sex is so emotional, it is also intimately connected to our identities. The wonderful part of that is that sex is so meaningful. The potential drawback is that it's all too easy for our sexuality to get damaged. Others can misuse and abuse us with horrible repercussions. Images from our own pasts can haunt us. Even society's ideas of sex can impact what we consider sexy.

Perhaps you're one of the lucky ones who has no problem feeling excitement for your husband and concentrating on him as you enjoy sex. If, instead, you're one of the majority of women who find that their pasts distort their sexuality, let's look at how God can bring hope and healing. Let's start by examining some of the most common threats to a godly sexuality.

Understanding the Danger of Pornography

Pornography, because it is so pervasive, is the most obvious example of something that can mar our sexuality. The point of pornography is to treat sex, and people, as if they exist merely for pleasure, and pleasure defined in a very narrow sense. Like lizards, we're supposed to just perform. We've thrown off the shackles of commitment so we are free to explore all our bodies have to offer, and in the process what have we become? Not more enlightened humans, but reptiles. We've actually gone backward.

The Problem for Her

Pornography, and the society that endorses these sorts of messages, can prevent us from enjoying a healthy sexual relationship. I vividly remember Laura, one of my counselors on a short-term mission trip when I was a teenager, warning all of us never to dabble in pornography, for as a small child she had seen some *Playboy* pictures, and twenty years later she was still unable to get them out of her head.

Laura's experience is not unique. Images have great power over our sexuality. Yet while these explicitly pornographic images can have long-term consequences, other things that we may not label pornographic can be almost as dangerous. Dr. Judith Reisman says that pornographic values have trickled down to the mainstream, where they can do even more harm.[1] Look at the covers of popular women's magazines. They may not be pornography, but they cause me to wonder if we should expand our definition. They teach us the same lies: sex is all about your body, and pleasure is all that matters.

Images have a way of defining our sexuality in a way that little else does. When the first images we have of sex, before our own sexuality is even really formed, are pornographic—even if it's "soft porn" like many magazine covers—we're going to think of sex as solely about physical pleasure.[2] In fact, we may find our ability to become aroused by love compromised, because love is not a part of what makes pornography sexy. The things that arouse us, instead, are impersonal depictions of sex.

For women hurt by this distortion, married sex isn't sexy. It's not pushing the envelope. It's as if you have a permission slip from your mom, and that takes all the fun out of it. The pornographic culture does not require fidelity, kindness, love, or even friendship. Many times people do not even have to know each other's names. Indeed, these things, which are so vital for a healthy sexual relationship, are actually considered *unsexy*, the very opposite of what sex is supposed to be. No wonder many of us have problems feeling desire for our husbands! For many women, desire is not shaped by a godly sexuality, even though they wish it was, and even though they may not consciously understand why it isn't.

All the things twenty-nine-year-old Belinda found sexy had nothing to do with actually being married. She often fantasized about things she had once read about that were very wrong. "I don't want any of these things to happen," she explained to me. "It's just that I can't get excited just thinking, *Oh, he's coming home tonight and we're going to make love.* It's nice, but it seems so tame. I don't want it to be that way, but when I decide not to think about any of my fantasies, I find I don't get excited." Sex in today's society is only sexy if it's somehow rebellious or forbidden, and what can be less forbidden than sex between two married, committed people?

We don't tend to think of people like Belinda as being typical, but Marnie Ferree, executive director of Bethesda Workshops, which helps sexual addicts find recovery, has found that 40 percent of addicts are actually female.[3] They compulsively struggle with pornography, masturbation, or even acting out; or, at the other end of the spectrum, they keep getting involved in destructive relationships. All find true intimacy out of their grasp, even if they want it desperately.

The Problem for Him

Though pornography can wreak havoc on your sexuality, it can also wreak havoc on your marriage if your husband avidly uses it. It's as if a wall goes up within the marriage, because instead of experiencing all the personal closeness we should during sex, we have to distance ourselves to become aroused.

Popular Christian vocalist Clay Crosse was courageous enough to tell others about his battle with lust after being exposed to pornography, because he wanted to help others avoid these dangers. His first encounter with pornographic pictures was at a friend's house when he was ten, and "they were burned into [his] brain."[4] Over the next few years he remembers several occasions where he again came in contact with similar materials. When he married his childhood sweetheart, he wasn't using pornography, but lust was a constant struggle for him because the images had shaped his sexuality. With God's help, he realized that he needed to surrender his thought life, even though it was immensely difficult.

Crosse's recovery was probably easier because he had given up pornography. Those who use it as adults have a much harder road because it becomes addictive. James Dobson was invited to interview serial killer Ted Bundy before Bundy was executed in 1989. Dobson reports that Bundy "shared with me how pornography pulled him out of a normal lifestyle and into a world of addiction and violence." He concludes, "Although many people are able to view pornography without following Bundy's murderous path, few are able to escape the mental and emotional scars that change their view of sexuality and jeopardize their ability to have normal relationships."[5]

Dr. Victor Cline from the University of Utah studied the stages people go through when they start using pornography, and it mirrors Bundy's spiral downward.[6] First is addiction; you become hooked and you keep going back to pornography, even if you don't want to. Next is escalation, when you start looking for more graphic images. Accompanying this is desensitization, when you begin to feel numb to what you see, and you need more and more graphic pornography to arouse you. Finally comes acting out, when you try to live out the images that are in your brain. Cline estimates that 8 percent of men and 3 percent of women are seriously addicted to pornography, a figure that is likely to increase since Internet porn is so readily available.

If your husband uses pornography, Marnie Ferree advocates refusing to have sex with him. Think of him like an alcoholic; you wouldn't offer an alcoholic a drink, so you shouldn't offer a pornography addict something that will feed his addiction, either. That may sound drastic, but he is committing adultery because he's lusting after somebody else, even if that person is just a picture (see Matt. 5:28). And the more he has sex with pornography in his mind, the harder it becomes for him to change. His brain actually becomes wired differently. It is not submission to watch pornography with him, either. It is sin, and you're hurting him and yourself in the process.

The purpose of this action, though, is not to punish him but to protect both of you. Therefore, it must be done in a loving way. If you start yelling at him—"I'm not going to have sex with you because you're a pervert!"—you're likely to make the situation worse. Instead, pray and go to someone else for help before you talk to him so you don't just blurt out threats. Visit a trained Christian counselor, someone who can support you in prayer and give you suggestions on how to talk with your husband about this problem. If you can't find a counselor, choose one wise friend who can give you prayer support. Do not, however, start talking to all your friends about the problem, even in the guise of "asking for prayer." It's being disrespectful to your husband, and when he does change, he will feel uncomfortable knowing that your acquaintances all knew of his problem.

Once you have the support, then talk with your husband and let him know why you've made this decision. Make it clear that you are more than willing to resume making love once he has stopped using pornography. Make sure that in other areas of your life you show him as much love and kindness as you can. Don't remind him about not doing the dishes, leaving his laundry on the floor, or other things that bother you. Let this be the main battle you are fighting today.

Overcoming Haunting Problems from the Past

The Destruction of Abuse

Whereas it can be difficult to erase pornographic images, it can seem impossible to erase abusive ones. When we're sexually abused, someone has violated the most personal, intimate parts of our lives. Little else can have such a horrifying effect.

These effects can be lifelong. Some women think they have been healed, only to be blindsided when all their feelings return in full force, perhaps at the birth of a daughter. Others never experience this dormancy. Some come to see sex in such negative terms they can't imagine ever wanting it, even if they deeply love their husbands. Others may become sexual addicts (and indeed, 80 percent of addicts report being sexually abused as children).[7] Still others recognize the power sex gives them and use it to punish men.

These reactions are not necessarily all conscious decisions. Yet any of them render making love freely to our husbands difficult. We're not ready to join ourselves emotionally in the act, even if we may emotionally feel all kinds of loving things for our husbands. Love and sex simply don't go together. Our bodies can't compute it.

Those Haunted by a Promiscuous Past

Sometimes the images in our head don't relate to what was done to us, but instead to what we did willingly. Today it's normal to experiment sexually long before people decide to commit. One opinion piece being debated widely around the Internet as I write this says premarital sex actually enhances marital happiness![8]

The author couldn't be more wrong. A study of 2,746 people in England found that those who had had premarital sex were 60 percent more likely to divorce, and far more likely to have affairs.[9] On the other hand, studies also show that people who follow God's design have the most physically enjoyable sex lives. One large-scale study found that 32 percent of conservative Protestant married women were likely to experience orgasm each and every time they had sex, a rate far higher than in any other group.[10] Even in the wider society, monogamous women are twice as likely to experience orgasm as promiscuous women, according to the famous *Redbook* study of 100,000 women.[11]

Sex is beautiful in its proper context, but when misused it prevents the very pleasure we yearn for. Here's how J. P. Crawley, one of my favorite Christian Internet bloggers,[12] responded to this debate over the dubious "benefits" of premarital sex:

> Sex binds two people whether they *want* to be bound or not. If no level of commitment is actually intended, if the bodies are "lying" to each other, then this will inevitably cause psychological confusion. This confusion can be acknowledged, denied, or repressed but it won't go away. Unless it is dealt with it will lead to psychological damage being done to the "response" mechanism. If the "sex equals commitment" message is overridden enough times, then eventually it loses any meaning at all. When one finally does enter into a committed relationship, sex will be simply an individual act of pleasure rather than a mechanism to bind two people into "one flesh."[13]

We've conditioned our minds to think of sex as only for pleasure, rather than for intimacy, ironically making it more difficult to experience that pleasure in a committed relationship. Even if we're committed to our marriages and regret our pasts, these pasts can still haunt us, intruding on our relationships now like a third person watching over us.

Those Who Were Raised to Be Prudish

Finally, there are those who suffer what is perhaps most endemic in the church: the underlying belief that sex must somehow be wrong. We're told from the time we're teenagers not to think about it, let alone do it. We need to keep ourselves pure, and thus as far away from sex as possible. Yet with the average age of first marriage increasing for women, many now have spent more than a decade before their wedding trying to suppress their sexual feelings. When we get married, we're so used to turning ourselves off that turning on isn't always easy.

But girls face an additional problem. Parents look at their son and think to themselves, *I can probably control him*. But when they look at their daughter, they realize they have to control not just her, but all the boys out there who may wish to "mess with her." Since that's impossible, they have to clamp down on their daughter even harder. Her sexuality becomes dangerous. Little girls are often yelled at if they touch their sexual organs, even if it's just out of harmless curiosity. This leaves a lasting impact. Think about how difficult it is for many women to say the word *vagina*, though men rarely have a problem with the word *penis*. We're taught that our bodies are somehow shameful, and we tend to internalize this far more than men do.

Reclaiming Godly Sexuality

Accepting Ourselves as God Does in Christ

These things we've been talking about—abuse, promiscuity, pornography, even prudishness—seem very different. And yet they share one common thread: they're all perversions of what God intended sex to be. They bind us with cords of guilt, shame, anger, even lust.

Even being saved may not necessarily mean we feel the freedom from these things that we so desperately want. Just because we're Christians doesn't mean we have allowed Christ into all the hidden recesses of our souls. One woman says, "I must have literally 're-ceived' Jesus hundreds of times but I never had any assurance that He actually came into my life."[14] The reason, as counselor Leanne Payne explains, is that God may live inside us, but that doesn't mean that we are necessarily whole.[15] We still may be cutting parts of ourselves off from Jesus' grace because we just can't deal with them ourselves.

One of the most profound things said about healing comes in the story of the Prodigal Son. He is eating the pigs' slop when he realizes his true condition. The Greek in Luke 15:17 literally says, "He came to himself." This may seem like pure semantics, but bear with me for a moment, because there's a very important principle expressed in these few words.

When sin entered the world, every human relationship was damaged. Most fundamentally, Adam and Eve were cut off from the perfect communion they had had with God. They were also cut off from each other, scapegoating each other for sin, and from the way God had made them to be. Sin fundamentally changed every human. As David wrote centuries later, "Surely I was sinful from the time my mother conceived me" (Psalm 51:5).

Yet even though we have sinned, we're still made in His image. We still have the unique personalities, the desire for spiritual things, and even the sexualities that He originally gave us. All of these things were made by God and are good and pure. Unfortunately, we can't enjoy them the way God intended because sin has marred them. God didn't create us to be marred like this. Those who choose wrong lifestyles distort, and can even almost destroy, the person that God intended us to be. But we can also damage that person, too, if we are taught to hate ourselves, through abuse or rejection (such as abandonment by a parent).

In Romans 7, Paul talks about this war that he has within himself.

Part of him wants to do right, but he just can't. It's like he's two different people. Many of us feel that way not only because we're tempted to sin, but also because we feel so ashamed of what's been done to us, or what we've done in the past, that we run away from that beautiful person God created us to be. Ultimately, we just don't feel we're that beautiful.

Healing, thus, is twofold. First, and most importantly, it's finding forgiveness and grace from God. It's stepping off of the treadmill we're running on, trying so hard to escape everything that has happened to us, and allowing God to make us new. It is realizing that Jesus not only died for all the sin we've ever done, but also for all the sin that's been done to us. But second, healing is coming back in contact with that person that God made us; the personalities, the gender, the sexuality, all those things that God gave to us that we may have rejected out of shame. That's difficult, because we're not used to who we're supposed to be. You see this most vividly in those with multiple personality disorder, who almost become different people in order to escape. The vast majority of us won't become different people like this, but we still might reject ourselves!

How do we accept ourselves again? Look out, because this is going to get messy. Purity isn't something a quick wipe down will accomplish; it has to be bought with blood. If you read through the Old Testament, and especially if you slog through Leviticus, you'll notice that purification wasn't pretty. It involved slaughtering some animal, boiling various parts of it, and sprinkling its blood, all to atone for the sins of the people. All of this was a foreshadowing of Christ's death on the cross, a grueling, horrific, torturous death that I don't think we can ever truly comprehend. Through that death our sins were washed away, and as Isaiah also tells us, "by his wounds we are healed" (Isaiah 53:5).

To achieve this kind of healing, we must be willing to face all the things that have happened to us in our lives, acknowledging how they have all molded our character and personality. Only by facing these things head on will we be able to begin to experience the wholeness we so desperately want. Integrating the abuse we suffered, or even our own past sins, with ourselves now isn't saying that these things define us. Instead, it's acknowledging that they are only a part of our story, one that God is still in the process of writing, and one that will, ultimately, have a very happy ending!

God is ready to lead you, if you will say with Jeremiah, "Heal me, O Lord, and I will be healed . . . for you are the one I praise" (Jer. 17:14). Many times, though, this grace is best ministered through another person. Seek out a friend, a pastor, or a counselor to pray with if you have really difficult issues that need to be resolved. Once we're able to find this acceptance and healing from God, our pasts won't affect our sex lives so much, and even the negative images we have can be erased. Let's see how.

Erasing Bad Pictures

Have you ever walked into a room and felt yourself, with a jolt, transported back twenty years to some starry night you haven't thought of for ages, simply because of the scent? Our brains remember things by making connections, and the more senses involved in the initial event, the firmer the connections are.

Sex involves an awful lot of senses, either for good or for bad. No wonder, then, that memories are likely to come flooding back unbidden when we're making love. Yet how can we erase these harmful memories so that we can enjoy our husbands as God intends? Those images are especially powerful when they are the first experiences we had feeling aroused (whether while being abused[17] or while viewing pornography as a young child). Some women may find those images necessary in order to become aroused, so that we can't even have sex without fantasizing.

God can help us with this problem because He promises that in Christ we are new creations (2 Cor. 5:17). However, we need to participate in this "re-creating" by accepting God's grace. We must break the ties that bind us to our old selves.

Leanne Payne, in her healing ministry, works backward with a person, looking at all the instances where forgiveness or repentance is

necessary (and sometimes both are needed simultaneously!), and giving these to God. Kathy, a sexual abuse survivor, explains how she
dealt with flashbacks in this way:

> Beginning with my molestation, we went prayerfully back to
> the very first circumstance involving my uncle and myself. Just
> to get to where I could face that event, we had to spend five or
> six afternoons in prayer together. With each incident I remem-
> bered, I re-entered the situation and told the Lord what I was
> feeling. Then I asked Him to forgive me for any feelings in me
> that were wrong. I also asked God to forgive the other person
> involved with me. And then, before God, I announced, as we
> completed praying through each scene, "And I forgive myself."
>
> I asked the Lord by His Holy Spirit to reveal memories that
> needed healing. . . . It was a painful process, but very worth-
> while. And even though I had already forgiven in the broad
> sense, I felt the need to give and receive forgiveness with a
> witness for each remembered incident.[18]

I had to go through a similar time of prayer in my marriage. Even
though I hadn't been abused, I had been rejected by the fathers and
father figures in my life, leaving a huge hole. When we were first
married, although I loved Keith I found it hard to trust him. We couldn't
figure out what the problem was, because I felt no animosity toward
him. One night as we were praying, I remembered a vow I had once
made that no man was going to get close enough again to hurt me. As
I prayed for forgiveness for that vow, released myself from it, and
forgave again the men who had abandoned me, we were able to experience a new level of intimacy in our marriage.

Kathy, too, was set free after prayer. Here's what she says:

> The inward change was soon obvious. Love, joy, peace—the
> very things I had longed for but never known for more than a
> few minutes at a time—became real for me. . . . The flashbacks
> ceased immediately. The healing I am describing happened

more than five years ago, and only twice in those five years have I ever again had a flashback. That abrupt change was inexplicable, because I had struggled with those memories all through the years. It was as though God erased a painful part of my memories.[19]

This kind of prayer is not something we can usually do alone. In most cases—though there are exceptions—it also isn't something a ten-minute huddle with God can accomplish, because you need to break down your heavy defenses so He can reveal things to you, minister to your spirit, and bring you to the place where you can forgive and know that you have been forgiven.

As long as we harbor anger, bitterness, or guilt, then that person or that sin still has power over us. It's not easy to forgive, and not easy to accept God's forgiveness, but it brings a freedom you can never imagine. If you're struggling, find someone mature and trustworthy to pray with, offer to God the images and fantasies that chain you, and let God set you free.

Being Present

Those with a distorted sexuality share another problem: they find it difficult to be present during sex. If you see sex as bad, especially if you were abused, you may distance yourself, thinking of anything else to distract you from what's happening. Others may need to fantasize about something else to be aroused. Part of healing, then, involves changing the way we make love. We must be present mentally and emotionally, and not just physically.

To do this, find things that focus your mind on what's occurring right now. Look him in the eye, talk to him, kiss him. Think about your body: What feels nice right now? What do you want him to do? What is he feeling? What can you do to make him feel great? Concentrate on the pleasure and intimacy that comes from you being together in this way.

Marnie Ferree recommends that if, in the middle of all of this, fantasies or images pop up again, you should tell your husband and then stop making love.[20] Pray about it together, and try again later. You may even need to take a hiatus to retrain your brain so that arousal and/or sex are not associated with negative things any more. It can be a long process, but it is speeded up as we are healed from the initial wounds.

However, you can slow down or even halt this healing process if you let new negative images in. If you are battling with flashbacks of pornography or other lovers, the worst thing you can do is to feed your mind with things that reinforce these problems. As Ferree says, "Feed the monster and it will keep growing." So here we go again: switch off that television! Most television shows turn sex into something purely carnal rather than something beautiful, and they will hurt your chances of winning the battle for godly sexuality. Clay Crosse found that it was the media that prevented him from winning the battle with lust for so long, because TV shows echoed what he had seen in magazines, even if they weren't as graphic. Don't feed on junk, and it will be easier to stop junk from surfacing.

Getting to "Very Good"

In the gospel of Luke, Jesus tells a story of a person being delivered from a demon. Afterward he was like a house that was all swept clean. A little while later, though, the demon returned to his old stomping ground, found the house empty, and invited seven more to move in with him. The end state of the man was worse than the first (Luke 11:26). The man was freed from the demon, but he didn't replace it with anything. His house was clean but empty. When we're trying to get rid of negative sexual patterns, we have to make sure we're replacing them with something new, too.

Knowing What God Thinks of Sex

Let's look at how God sees sex. This question can be partly answered with reference to one female body part: the clitoris. There is no purpose to this little knob of flesh, with more nerve endings than any other part of the body, except to give a woman pleasure. In some African cultures, societies fear this capacity of women so much that they conduct a brutal surgery on little girls to remove it, to make sure girls don't enjoy sex so they won't be promiscuous. But God created sex to feel good.

He also created sex to express the mystical union that Christ has with the church. Not only are our bodies joined, but also our souls. Isn't it amazing that this is also how children are made? They are produced when we are joining together intimately, reaffirming for each other the commitment and love that will be needed to provide for a family.

Sex, then, is not something to be ashamed of, but at the same time it's a private thing. It's a secret between you and your husband. It reaffirms the unique nature of your relationship every time you join together.

If you know all these things in your head, but have a hard time accepting them, don't despair! We're told in Romans 12:2 that we're supposed to renew our minds, not our feelings, so let's fill our minds with Scripture that tells us truths about sex and who we are today. Here are some verses to get you started:

- The sexual relationship is part of marriage, it was part of the perfect creation, and it is nothing to be ashamed of:

  For this reason a man will leave his father and mother and be united to his wife, and they will become one flesh. The man and his wife were both naked, and they felt no shame. (Gen. 2:24–25)

- God approved of everything He made—including our sexuality:

  And God saw all that he had made, and it was very good. (Gen. 1:31)

- Women, too, can be sexual beings and have input into their sexual relationships:

The wife's body does not belong to her alone but also to her husband. *In the same way, the husband's body does not belong to him alone but also to his wife.* (1 Cor. 7:4, emphasis added)

- Erotic love is good:

Let him kiss me with the kisses of his mouth—for your love is more delightful than wine. (Songs 1:2, along with the rest of the book)

Too often we overlook the second part of this verse. This was revolutionary: women had equal rights in a marriage! And men were not to abuse their wives' bodies with their own.

- Our sexual relationship is to be fun and enjoyable well into later years:

May your fountain be blessed, and may you rejoice in the wife of your youth. A loving doe, a graceful deer—may her breasts satisfy you always, may you ever be captivated by her love. (Prov. 5:18–19)

- We don't need to define ourselves by what was done to us, or by what we have done in the past:

Therefore, if anyone is in Christ, he is a new creation; the old has gone, the new has come! (2 Cor. 5:17)

- We don't need to be confined to the negative behavior patterns that have trapped us:

But thanks be to God that, though you used to be slaves to sin, you wholeheartedly obeyed the form of teaching to which you were entrusted. You have been set free from sin and have become slaves to righteousness. (Rom. 6:17–18)

- God can forgive and forget any sin that we confess:

  As far as the east is from the west, so far has he removed our transgressions from us. (Ps. 103:12)

Those of you who have been abused probably need something a little more: a vision of God loving you and being with you, even as you were abandoned, abused, or rejected. Think about these:

- God gets really angry when anyone hurts a child:

  And if anyone causes one of these little ones who believe in me to sin, it would be better for him to be thrown into the sea with a large millstone tied around his neck. (Mark 9:42)

- God can heal us:

  Heal me, O Lord, and I will be healed; save me and I will be saved, for you are the one I praise. (Jer. 17:14)

- God comes to the rescue of those who have been abandoned:

  A father to the fatherless, a defender of widows, is God in his holy dwelling. (Ps. 68:5)

Commit to memory the verses that speak most to you. If we start focusing on godly sexuality, we won't be haunted by a perverted one anymore. Instead of lying down and letting our pasts roll over us, we will be standing up and fighting with truth. And we will be able to say with confidence, like Jeremiah, "Heal me and I will be healed."

For Him

Earlier we learned that your wife is an alien. Today's lesson is similar: you are not a lizard. That may seem obvious, but with the way sexuality is portrayed in our culture, it sure seems as if we're supposed to resemble reptiles rather than humans created in God's image: we see a mate, and we procreate. Sex in pornography, in movies, or on the covers of magazines is something purely physical rather than something rich with emotion and love.

As a man, you likely struggle with maintaining purity. Men are visually stimulated, and it's easy to become addicted to pornography or lust. If you're going to have a healthy sexual relationship, though, you must not give in to this temptation. First, it's sin, pure and simple. But pornography also debases women and erases the emotional component from sex. What's sexy is not married sex, where you express intimacy sexually (what C. S. Lewis termed Eros), but sex with an anonymous stranger. Lewis put it this way: "Sexual desire, without Eros, wants *it, the thing in itself;* Eros wants the Beloved."[21]

If you're haunted by images from pornography, or you have a hard time seeing marriage as sexy, then pray for a renewed love for your wife, and vow not to give in to pornography or lust. This may require censoring the TV programs and movies you watch so as to avoid reinforcing negative ideas about sex. It may even require attending a support group or talking to a counselor. Finally, read some verses that celebrate how wonderful sex is in its proper context. You can find some earlier in this chapter.

Pornography isn't the only thing that can mar our sexuality. Some of us were also abused as children. If you were, talk to a counselor. If your wife was, be patient with her. A most delicate part of her was damaged, and she needs to trust you before she can give it to you.

God made sex because He wants us to enjoy it. It's precious. But think of how you treat other precious things. Men who collect antique cars polish them, wax them, and watch for any blemish or problem so they can take care of it before it gets out of control. They're constantly vigilant. We need to have the same attitude about sex. It's precious, it's fragile, and it needs our tender care so that it can shine, too.

Chapter 5

R-E-S-P-E-C-T

"W ill he still respect me in the morning?" is a question we hear in movies, usually asked at rather inopportune times. Yet for real-life women, perhaps a more pertinent question is, "Does he respect me now?" After all, if a woman feels like he wants her just for her body, but not because of the relationship, sex can feel cheap. Who wants to give herself to a man who doesn't truly respect her?

When we're talking about respect, we don't mean respect for *doing* something, either. He may respect your chosen profession, or your ability to do two loads of laundry while you get the children ready for school, or your willingness to cook Christmas dinner for fifteen relatives you haven't seen all year. But does he respect you for who you are?

Our Need to Matter

Being able to answer yes to that question is crucial for intimacy. But perhaps you just don't feel as if he always respects your point of view or your feelings. When he decides what to do, he doesn't seem to take you into account.

Here's the good news. Even if you don't feel like you make a difference to him, studies show that you do! Single men are far more likely to engage in self-destructive behaviors than married men. Married men steer clear because they care what their wives think, and they don't want to endanger that relationship.[1]

Married men also spend far less time with "the guys" than do single men, even those who are living with their girlfriends. Married men stay home more and talk to the women in their lives more than the cohabiting men do.[2] They do care. It may not be as much as you would like, but most likely he has changed at least a little to accommodate you.

But what if that's not enough? You need more. You want him to show you vividly that he respects you. Feeling his respect, though, is a two-way street. Certainly he has to respect you, but you also have to believe that he does. And the problem is not always completely with him.

Our Roadblocks to Respect

"I Feel Lousy, So You Must Think I'm Lousy, Too!"

I've always been a stay-at-home mom, but I haven't always been at peace with it. A few years ago, when my girls were toddlers, it seemed that my mission in life was to make sure that everyone knew how much I had sacrificed. It wasn't that I didn't enjoy being with my daughters; there was nowhere else I would rather have been. But ultimately I was afraid that I was losing the respect I could have had if I had taken a job. It was significantly easier to feel respected when my creativity and problem solving skills were applied to something other than how to remove peanut butter from long blonde hair or how to find yet another use for dry macaroni.

So when Keith complained—at times justifiably—that the house was a mess or that I was always miserable, I would argue that there was no way he could possibly understand, because all day at work people told him how brilliant he was. I got to mop up when my kids missed the potty.

I felt he didn't respect me, but in retrospect, I can see how unreasonable I was being. At the time, the feeling was very real that he didn't understand enough what I was sacrificing for the family. I'm not exactly sure, though, what steps he could have taken to persuade me that he did, in fact, understand. I wanted to feel like the wronged partner. If I couldn't get the rewards of working at a good job, at least I could get the rewards of knowing that I was morally superior.

It was only when Keith challenged me to get a job that I began to do some painful soul-searching. I realized that I had been striving to find the affirmation from others that ultimately I could only find in God. This came as a big surprise to me, because I thought I trusted God with everything. When my father and then later my stepfather left me as a child, I determined that God was enough. When my son died, again I knew God was with me, and He carried me through.[3]

Yet even though God was enough for all the big things in my life, I wouldn't let Him be enough for the little things. I didn't trust Him for my peace and fulfillment on a daily basis, in the middle of Cheerios and mashed bananas. I could trust Him in a graveyard; I couldn't in the kitchen. And when I eventually confessed this to God, my outlook on life changed. I stopped being so miserable. I was still just as busy, often just as tired, and just as in need of encouragement from my husband as I was before. Nevertheless, I stopped needing constant reinforcement that I was the best.

I tell that story not to say how enlightened I am now, but to encourage you to ask whether the lack of respect you feel from your husband is entirely his fault. There are times when husbands are insensitive to their wives. (Don't worry; we'll deal with that soon.) Sometimes, though, we're the ones with unrealistic demands.

As we talked about in chapter 1, women seem to have a greater need than men do to be viewed as the sacrificial ones in the relationship, because it encourages men to stay. But if we're always dwelling on what he owes us, we're expecting something from him that he can never really give. Is God big enough for your kitchen? Can you feel how worthwhile you are in His eyes, regardless of what society may say about your choices? No one can ultimately make you feel worthwhile except for God.

"I'm Not Very Exciting"

Some of us, though, haven't internalized this lesson. We don't believe we're worth much, and often it shows! Have you ever walked into a crowd of people you don't know? Usually within a minute or two you have figured out who the most important or popular people are. Often it's not because anyone has announced it; instead, these individuals act as if it's natural to have others flock to them. They're used to having respect.

Many of us act as if we don't deserve respect. We act instead as if we are shame-filled.[4] At home, we rarely speak our minds, or make suggestions, or even challenge our husbands when they're doing something wrong. On some level, we don't think our opinions are worth much. We think we have little to offer, and we act in such a way as to encourage our husbands to think that, too. After all, what's enticing about somebody who can recite *The Cat in the Hat* or all of the Veggie Tales movies? Or perhaps you're at the other end of the spectrum, and you're wondering what's enticing about a middle-aged woman with crow's feet who never had a professional job? You see all the women your husband is with all day and you don't think you measure up. This is a sure recipe for disaster in your sex life, let alone the other aspects of your marriage, because sex involves opening up and sharing yourself with your husband. If you don't feel like you have anything worth sharing, you may hold back, so that you're not able to throw yourself into making love.

Yet you do have something worth sharing. God made you unique; He planned you just the way you are (Psalm 139). You are worthwhile to Him, and you are worthwhile to your husband. He did, after all, marry you for a reason! Being worthwhile doesn't mean that we have to be the stereotypical superwoman, either. You may not know what the Dow closed at today or what the top headlines of the *New York Times* were, but you can still be exciting to be with. Knowing a certain set of facts is not what attracts people. We don't want people who are trying hard to be interesting; we want people who are *interested,* who are excited about life. When someone is passionate about something, even if we don't share that particular passion, we find that passion itself is contagious, especially in a marriage. What excites you? Whether it's quilting, investing, studying Scripture, making an impact on your community, or something else, pursue it. Your husband may look up in surprise one day at this amazing woman he married, and light a fire in your bedroom you've never experienced before!

"I Can't Stop Worrying About My Husband with Other Women"

When we're feeling as if everybody else has more to offer than we do, it's easy to slip into jealousy. You may start to notice who your husband is talking to, or wonder what he's doing at work, building up threatening scenarios in your mind. Quite likely he's not actually thinking about other women, but you may assume he is because you project your own feelings of inadequacy. When husbands realize this, another wedge can grow. Let's face it: people who are unjustifiably jealous aren't attractive. Nevertheless, many of us are dealing with very real feelings. How can we reassure ourselves that our husbands still love us?

In the next chapter, we'll talk about ways to build our friendship and our relationship, which can alleviate these fears. First, though, let's remind ourselves that God loves us. When we realize how worthwhile we are to God, we're less likely to project our fears onto our husbands. Understanding our worth can also affect how we act.

That doesn't mean you'll necessarily become a natural at parties; it does mean that you can radiate peace within yourself because you know God. When you feel comfortable with yourself, others will usually feel comfortable with you, too, and that definitely includes your husband!

On the other hand, perhaps your husband has given you good reason to be jealous. He comments favorably on how other women look. He stays at work late. He goes on lunch dates. Maybe he even had an affair in the past, and you wonder how you can ever trust him again.

As much as possible, be involved in his life. Go to work functions. Play hostess and get to know his colleagues. Talk to the women in his workplace, not to "scope them out," but so that you can start to see them as people and not just threats. When your married life is incorporated into his work life, it will be harder for him, too, to draw a distinct line between the two and find his allegiance straying.

If he does have an affair, get hold of some good books on how to deal with this (see the resources section at the back of this book. You *will not* bring him back by being more romantic and enticing. He needs a taste of what he'll be missing without you: a cold, hard dose of reality, not the feel of you snuggling against him to try to win him back.

Their Roadblocks to Respect

We've seen how we can erect roadblocks so that we don't feel respect and love. Now let's look at the other side of the equation: what to do when your husband and even your kids don't treat you with respect.

"He Doesn't Value What I Do!"

I laughed when I read a recent study done in Europe about women's time commitments and how those commitments affected their sex lives. In Italy, women have made great strides in the workforce. Yet their progress at home has lagged behind that of other Western European nations, mostly because their culture is one in which men tend to take their wives for granted. So today, when an Italian woman comes home, she still does most of the housework. She is run off of her feet, and the end result is that she spends less time on sex than do women in Finland, Sweden, or England.[5] Italian men, who are known for their machismo, aren't actually getting as much loving as English men are, largely because culturally they have not yet learned to respect women's contributions.

We may not be as undervalued as our Italian sisters are, but we're still often taken for granted. It's hard for many men to respect what we do because they themselves weren't reared for it and would never do it. Women typically do the lion's share of the housework, so it's assumed we're not as important as the men are, since they're able to escape the drudgery. You may even buy into some of this mentality, wondering who you are since you're "just a mother" or "just a wife." Ultimately, though, everything will pass away except people. The impact we have on our kids or our neighbors is perhaps even more important than any job we could have, and this impact is only possible because of the work we do at home, whether or not we also have a job.

If your husband diminishes the value of what you do, then he perceives value outside of Christ. Have a family meeting and talk about where you're going as a family. How does he want the children raised? What does he want for the family in the long run? What values does he want your children to have? How are they going to develop them? Many people have never answered these questions. They go through life working at their jobs without asking the reason behind what they're doing. Throw everything on the table: his job, your job, your kids' schooling, all your commitments and activities, and ask God for a vision for your family. Once you both have one, it's easier for you as a couple to see how everyone's labor, wherever it's done, fits into that vision.

Even if your husband isn't a believer, you can still discuss where your family is heading. Brainstorm about how you can make sure your family meets the goals you set. Chances are this will involve valuing the typical things we women do, like creating a comfortable home and nurturing the children. Once you've verbalized the importance of your contribution, it's easier for him to want to be involved around the house, or, at the very least, to be grateful that you are!

"Everyone Thinks I'm the Maid!"

Sometimes we don't get respect because we don't act like we should. Respect is not something we can demand. We can demand obedience, but we cannot demand respect. Respect is a voluntary act of the will.

If we want respect, we have to act in a way that others would respect. This message hasn't been explained enough in the church. The Bible certainly tells us to "serve one another in love" (Gal. 5:13). Some may interpret this to mean we are to allow others to demand from us, even to demean us. But Scripture also tells us that we are of infinite worth to God; that every hair of our heads is numbered (Luke 12:7). Jesus came to earth as a servant, but He didn't cease being the Son of God. When He washed the disciples feet, He showed He would do lowly things, but that didn't mean He was worthless. As women, we do lots of lowly things, too: washing underwear, cleaning toilets, wiping noses. But that doesn't have to mean that we are less important than those we serve. Does serving mean that we completely sacrifice all our needs? Can we reconcile serving and earning respect when we consider how we should treat others?

Philippians 2:4 says this: "Each of you should look not only to your own interests, but also to the interests of others." Notice that nowhere does it say we are to *ignore* our legitimate needs, just that we are to consider others'. I think this relates to the purpose of servanthood. The thing God cares about most is bringing people closer to Him (John 3:16–17). He wants people to be like Christ (Rom. 8:29). That means that as His servants, this should be our primary goal, too. True servanthood should point people toward Christ. Sometimes, though, we forget about this principle. In *To Love, Honor, and Vacuum* I explained it this way.

> If we pamper our children, they will not feel responsible for their own messes, their own actions, and even more far-reaching, their own mistakes. They may grow into adults feeling a good life is owed to them without effort, or may engage in hazardous activities without thinking of what may happen. If we do the same for our husbands, the chance at having a marriage relationship characterized by mutual respect and admiration is severely limited. . . . [And if] your husband and children do not respect you, it will be very hard for you to model Christ to them.[6]

When we routinely do things for people that they should do for themselves, we allow them to treat us in an un-Christlike manner. When your ten-year-old son comes in from school, drops his backpack on the floor and throws his coat on a chair, and then goes and plays Nintendo while you clean up, you teach him to treat you with disrespect. You ingrain patterns of selfishness that will become harder to unravel as he grows older. This is not serving.

Does this mean that we should never pick up after our children or clean up after our husbands? Of course not. But we need to judge what we do by its effects on our relationships. If people are acting selfishly, it's because they are rewarded for it. Servanthood should not be a cover for others' selfishness. But even worse, if our family members don't respect us, how can they think we have any useful opinions or advice? How can we model Christ or encourage godly behavior if they learn to disregard us?

If husbands and children are to respect us, then, it's important to keep in mind the lessons of Galatians 6. In verse 2, Paul exhorts us to "carry each other's burdens," but in verse 5, he goes on to say "each should carry his own load." Is this inconsistent? Not if you look at the Greek. The words for "burden" and "load" are different. *Load* is one's daily allowance, what a person may be expected to carry. *Burden* is something one person cannot carry alone. If you are carrying everybody's loads, you won't have any energy to carry their genuine burdens. And your husband and children will be so used to discarding any excess baggage that it won't occur to them to pick up the occasional burden or two, as well!

In 1 Thessalonians 5:14, Paul tells us to "warn those who are idle, encourage the timid, help the weak." The ones we are to warn are the idle, those who are not carrying their load. When people fail to do for themselves what they should, they expect someone else to do it for them. It's a sign of self-centeredness, exactly the opposite of Christlike servanthood.

Many argue that it's wrong for women to want to be respected or to "demand" rights, and in one sense this is true—if we're pushing for them out of pride. But even Paul, whose life is an example of servanthood, demanded his rights as a Roman citizen when he was tossed into jail and his ability to witness was at stake (Acts 16:37). Within the family unit, it's all too easy to lose our ability to witness when we are not respected. This will also damage our own psyche, our kids' abilities to form functional relationships now and into adulthood, and our marriages.

While we want to protect ourselves and our families from this, it's still a fine line to cross. In daily life, what's the difference between a burden and a load? And how can we make sure we're acting appropriately without starting a big fight? Each family will answer these questions differently.

If you stay at home and your husband works outside the home, he will not be able to do as much housework as you will. It is your job to carry part of his burden, perhaps by making most meals, doing the laundry, or doing most of the cleaning. But if you are also constantly retrieving his dirty underwear from beside the hamper, or holding dinner for him when he's late (even when he doesn't call), you are accepting too much of his *load*. Whether he's doing it consciously or not, he's treating you as someone not worthy of respect, and that diminishes your value in his eyes, as well as your own. It also diminishes your value in the eyes of your children, who learn that it's okay to take advantage of Mom.

Confronting him with these issues, though, must be done out of an attitude of love, and not to demand justice. Perhaps this is where servanthood is best modeled. The purpose is to point him to God, not bash him on the head with condemnation. If you have been going through a rough time, it may be better to wait to confront him. After all, God doesn't confront us with all of our faults at one time, so we shouldn't do that to our husbands, either! Changing the little things we do on a daily basis, though, is a step we can take now to build a house—and a marriage—modeled on respect.

"My Kids Don't Respect Me!"

Feeling respect from the man you make love to is vital to a healthy sex life, but creating other respectful relationships also builds our sense of self and lowers our stress level. Perhaps nowhere is this as important as with our children. We love them more intensely than anyone else, and if these relationships are broken, our sexuality will be marred because our souls are scarred.

That's why the principle of carrying one's own load is vital for children to learn. Unfortunately, it's becoming a far less common lesson. Children's work was once necessary for the family. The whole reason that we have summer vacation, after all, is because kids were needed on the farm. Today few children even do chores, and God warns us that this is disastrous. The idle get a distorted view of the world. If we excuse our kids from doing anything productive, they can easily feel as if the world revolves around them: people clean for them, chauffeur them to activities, supervise their play dates, and give them spending money. Why listen to your parents' values and morals, or even their spiritual beliefs, if you are the center of the universe?

If you're battling with this issue at home right now, try to find an older Christian couple to mentor you, people who have already lived through the challenges that you face now. I don't have room here to give a philosophy of parenting, but let me stress two things: first, children must be productive in the house and they need to learn that they have purpose and are valuable. Ironically, letting kids run around free can actually be detrimental.

Second, being strict is not the same thing as being loud. Many parents yell and make threats—"You stop hitting your sister this instant or you won't watch TV for a month!"—so they think they're strict. But if they never follow through, children will learn to disregard what they say, while the volume in the house steadily increases. What a blueprint for stress!

So don't yell, and don't threaten. Do something. This isn't foolproof, and children can always choose to go astray even with the best of parents. Adam, after all, had God as a Father, and he still wandered. Yet anything we can do to reduce our stress by ensuring that our kids listen to us will build our self-confidence and the harmony in our family, and thus, by extension, the harmony in our bedroom.

God has put inside each of us real needs for relationship and community. Ultimately our needs for affirmation can only be met in Him, but He designed human relationships to model His relationship with us. Find your worth in God first, and then build relationships that reflect His values. As you do so, you'll build a family that cares about each other and loves life. You'll feel more confident, more at peace, and more inclined to share yourself in the bedroom!

For Him

Don't end up like Italian men! A recent study in Italy found that Italian women feel profoundly unappreciated by their husbands, so they watch TV rather than having sex. If you want to spice up your love life, you need to pick up a mop, or at least say "thank you" when your wife does.

I know it seems like you have to jump through hoops to get your wife to love you, but this is something that's important. It's easy to take someone for granted when she seems willing to do a lot of work around the house that you'd rather not do anyway. But you can take several steps to make her feel better.

1. Respect her. She has to spend her life doing dirty laundry, washing dirty dishes, and cleaning up after everyone else. Maybe you don't have the time to do a lot of these tasks (if you do, then think about doing your share!), but you can make sure that you at least don't make things harder for her. If you have a cup of coffee, don't leave the cup for her to clean up. Don't leave your dirty laundry on the floor for her to pick up. She probably doesn't mind doing the dishes or the laundry, but you'd lighten her mood considerably if you made it easy for her!

2. Say thanks. When you get in the door, and she looks really tired, find something you can compliment. Say that you can't believe she managed to make dinner given how busy her day must have been, or compliment her on keeping the living room clean. Notice what she did do instead of what she didn't have time for. It will make a world of difference.

3. Often we treat those who are closest to us the worst. Try to reverse that. Treat her better than you treat anyone else: your boss, your mother, or your best friend. The more you build emotional intimacy, the more you're likely to build physical intimacy.

4. I've also told her that sometimes we women are the problem. We don't stand up for ourselves, especially with the kids. We think we don't deserve respect if we don't work outside the house. Your wife may think you're disrespecting her, when it's really that she has low self-esteem! I've asked her to pray about these issues, too.

Chapter 6

You Don't Bring Me Flowers

Dan may not have bought Renee a blender for their anniversary, but he didn't do much better. He started off well, hiring a babysitter and taking his wife on a two-hour trip to the big city, where he dined her in style. Then, just when Renee was waiting for the grand finale—a play or a concert—he took her to three hours' worth of *Saving Private Ryan*. Dan had a wonderful time and couldn't figure out why his wife seemed less than enthusiastic. I mean, come on, the good guys won!

Renee isn't the most flowery of women. She lives in a house full of testosterone, since most of the oldest children are male. She has organizing her children's schedules down to an art form. But inside her is still a woman who, like many of us, yearns for a little romance.

Men, on the other hand, just want to understand what we mean by "romance" so they can get to the more important task at hand. Dan thought he was accomplishing it by arranging for a date night, but he failed on the "romance usually does not involve graphic violence" front. To men like Dan, women can seem pathetically mushy. After all, we melt over and over again at things as predictable as flowers or chocolates. But we know it isn't about the tokens themselves (though a good box of chocolate truffles will go a long way in my book); it's because of what they represent. Our desire for romance is, at heart, a desire for relationship.

Romance for a husband means paying attention to making his wife feel pampered and special, so that any physical intimacy that follows is an expression of how precious the two are to each other. What may be romantic to one woman may not do a thing for somebody else, either. There is no perfect romantic plan. But if we all acknowledge that relationship is our underlying need, then we can see how important romance is for getting us "in the mood." After all, if romance is never a part of our lovemaking, then it's as if anybody could be in our place. Add the romance, and he's showing that he cares about *you*— that he's thinking about what you want and need (even if it does seem like he's only doing it to get to the grand prize).

It's completely unromantic to dissect romance, of course, but that's what we're going to do in this chapter. Romance is supposed to "just happen," but waiting for Dan to choose *My Big Fat Greek Wedding* over *Saving Private Ryan* may mean Renee's going to spend her life in a romance black hole. Like Dan, your husband may never comprehend this on his own. That doesn't mean, though, that you have to live without romance! If you understand what your real needs are, you can transform your relationship so that it meets these needs, even if not in the way you once dreamed.

Romance Means Relationship

Romance, the way we typically mean it, can be broken down into two different elements. The first element is the effort to make each other feel special. Time spent connecting, discussing each other's days, and sharing dreams can all increase our romance quotient. But then there are the other elements of romance: the outside trappings, the things that remind us that sex is not just physical, but also emotional, like the flowers, the scented candles, or the luxurious bubble bath. These extras make us feel sensuous, relaxed, and ready to think about the more amorous ways we can use our bodies.

Most women need both of these aspects of romance. That "Me-Tarzan-You-Jane" approach to relationships wears out pretty quickly. But perhaps you're married to a Tarzan who sees no need to come out of the trees. He spends his life showing off his manly traits by flying among all the other apes. He wants you to be so overpowered by his masculinity that you want to climb up that tree to get to him.

Every marriage needs encounters like that. Love does not always have to involve flowers and candles and long, drawn-out seductions. A Tarzan-Jane episode every now and then can help make him feel like he's still enough to entice you even without all the extras—and indeed, he may see the need for all that extra stuff as an insult to his ability to excite you. After all, he looks at you and is instantly attracted; why can't you feel the same way about him?

Yet most women understand an important relationship truth that men may not grasp as easily. You know how much more meaningful, intense, and intimate making love can be when it is accompanied by making an effort to encourage the relationship on other levels as well. In Song of Songs, love "is as strong as death." It "burns like a blazing fire, like a mighty flame" (8:6). Love can be so amazing it almost consumes you. So how are you going to get your Tarzan down out of that tree so you can experience this blaze?

Building the Tree Fort

Seeing Things from His Lookout

Though we may wish for romance in which we're the ones pampered and appreciated, increasing our romance quotient may require that we start the pampering ourselves. This isn't easy, especially if you're waiting to be swept off your feet. In fact, you may need to let go of this dream of your night in shining armor if you're ever going to have that relationship that's central to romance. We women have a hard time letting go of these expectations, though. It's estimated that a woman buys a Harlequin romance novel every five seconds.[1] But does this help romance or hurt it? If we're always wishing for something more, and something so out of the realm of our husband's universe that we're light years apart, we may never be satisfied in our marriages. He will sense this judgment and pull away.

Don't feed your mind with romance novels, soap operas, or other harmful illusions that will just make you chronically unsatisfied. Take the initiative yourself to warm up the relationship to romance. Instead of waiting for him to make you feel special, you can reach out to your husband so that he feels more inclined to reach back. But when you're reaching out, you have to do it in a way that speaks his language.

Women have an internal "false flattery meter." Probably little riles you more than asking your husband for an honest assessment of your appearance before going out to dinner, only to have him pronounce you gorgeous without even glancing up. Then, halfway through the evening, you discover that your slip is showing. He didn't even try to help you.

Sometimes we do similar things to our beloveds without realizing it when we don't try to understand their point of view. I like saying, "I love you," and my family members probably hear those words dozens of times a week. To me, these rich words mean a host of things, from "I would marry you all over again" (to my husband) to "I cherish you" (to my kids). But when Keith hears "I love you," a voice inside his head asks, "Why?" Hearing "I love you" is perfectly sufficient for me, but it doesn't mean as much to him, and can even cause self-doubt. But thanking him for specific things—"I love the way you stuck up for me with that insurance agent"—makes him feel ten feet tall.

What makes your husband tick? What is he particularly worried about recently, and how can you express your support for him through it? Maybe you can say how proud you are to be married to someone who is so hard working. This may not be something that you think is most important in a marriage, but he probably values it highly and takes his responsibility very seriously. Do you tell him you appreciate it? By affirming him for the things he values, you show that you understand him. You build the foundation for that tree fort where your Tarzan will want to kick back and relax with you.

Sharing His Jungle Vine

Instead of standing at the bottom of the tree yelling up to him about how great the grass feels down here, let's put on our boots and climb up that tree ourselves. It doesn't help to nag him about your need to spend more time together if he's just not interested.

Have you ever tried to convince him to hire a baby-sitter so you can go to dinner alone, or to agree to go on a Marriage Encounter weekend, or even to walk around the block with you, only to have him throw up any number of excuses? According to him, that's a waste of time, a waste of money, and there's no point because your marriage is fine anyway.

Frustration can drive us crazy, along with very real feelings of rejection and loneliness. However, these activities, though worthy, are all attempts to get him to do what *we* want to do. Sometimes a better approach is to meet on his turf. My friend Derek is a hunter. Every year, he and his wife Lisa go to his hunting camp together. It may not seem like a typically romantic thing to do, but they're alone nonstop for several days, they share an adventure, and they laugh in their rustic cabin with no electricity.

Changing the Scenery

This may work for Lisa, but perhaps you think your husband is a hopeless case. Emily, another friend, says her problem is not that they don't share interests; it's that her husband doesn't seem to have any interests in the first place. Ask her what Peter does in his leisure time, and she'll reply "work." Emily laments the fact that they spend no time together as a family, let alone as a couple. For the first few years of their marriage, Emily pressured him to carve out time together. Although he would agree, he always seemed to do so grudgingly. In his mind, she was taking him away from what he *should* be doing. He was neglecting his duty.

What they both needed was a change of scenery—a different perspective. One day Emily sat down and looked at it from his point of view. Peter was always worried about money. He felt that his job as a husband was to provide, especially since their family kept expanding. Emily was quite happy to live on less if it meant that he was home more often, but he interpreted being home as laziness. Instead, she decided to do everything she could to show him that she felt he was a good provider and that their family was prospering. She worked to make their money stretch, so they could have nice things without needing as much cash. She shopped at second-hand stores for the kids' clothes, she wrote out grocery lists and bought only what they needed, and she checked for sales. Most of all, Emily stopped saying out loud how much she wished they owned something or other, or how she wanted to redo the kitchen, or even how she admired the clothes that other women wore. Even though she never said these things out of jealousy, her husband interpreted these comments as evidence of his failure to provide. Instead, she started saying, "Isn't it wonderful how we have enough money for music lessons," and "Did you see the lovely Christmas outfits I was able to get for the kids today?"

The other element of her plan involved taking some financial responsibility for family activities. She began putting aside money each week from her grocery fund, and a year later she had enough for a vacation. All of this didn't completely change Peter. He still worked weekends, he still considered it his primary goal in life to provide for his family rather than to nurture his relationship with them, and he still would choose to work in the garage rather than come inside and play with their children. But he gradually began to agree to go out more with Emily and to take a vacation together. When Emily started to adjust to his point of view, he found it easier to adjust to hers. She had climbed up that tree, and now he was willing to explore new areas with her.

Many of us have husbands like Peter who work so much that time together seems harder to find than homework two minutes before the school bus arrives. If your husband doesn't understand how much the family needs *him*, and not just his wallet, try having that conversation we talked about earlier. Choose a time when you're not angry so that you can toss ideas around together. Ask him where he would like to be in five years or ten years, not just with his job, but also with his kids, with you, with God. And then brainstorm about how you can take steps to make sure he gets there. How can you make sure that he gets time to coach Little League, or to go to all his daughter's dance recitals? Don't tell him what he *should* think, but let him vocalize his own ideas.

It may take him a while to understand how relationships need an investment of time. This isn't always a bad process, though it can drive us nuts living through it. In the Song of Songs, Solomon invites the Shunammite to come away with him now that the winter and rain are over. He is ready and eager for their relationship now; he wasn't before. Sometimes we need to be careful to wait until our husbands are ready, too.

Football coach Bill McCartney's wife, Lyndi, had to wait for thirty years before her husband clued in to what he was missing by dedicating everything to his job and little to his family. When he did, he surprised the sports community by resigning at the height of his career, just because he realized how his selfishness had hurt his wife. But, ironically, they both needed that valley experience—though Bill, at the time, didn't interpret it as a valley—to grow in Christ and ultimately form such strong marriage bonds. Even if your prayers seem unending, God can work.

This doesn't mean that we can't nudge our husbands in the right direction; only that nagging and lecturing will not cause someone to change his whole outlook on life. And many men have a distorted picture of what is valuable in life, as Bill McCartney once did. They have inadvertently sacrificed their families on the altar of work, not even realizing what they were doing.

Often there's a family pattern to this behavior. Many men who are workaholics also have fathers who were workaholics, or some other kind of "holic." They resent missing out on time with their own dads, but they don't know how to be different. Yet the McCartney's story offers hope to all of us. After realizing he was neglecting his family, Bill formed Promise Keepers to help men be husbands first. If there's a Promise Keepers rally in your area, see if any of your husband's friends are going, and encourage him to go along, too.

Some of our husbands, no matter how much we try to support them, will never reciprocate and support us. It's a fallen world. You can take the steps I lay out here, but ultimately it's his decision, though it's so hard to leave something that impacts your life so much in someone else's hands! But you can't change him; God has to. Often He does this through the influence of other men. When Laura, fifty, was worried about her husband, she arranged for a man from church to help him with a handyman project. They spent a week sawing and hammering together, and in the process talked about many things of great importance (and many that were not!). Perhaps there are couples you think could help you and your husband, as well. Have them over for dinner, join their small group at church, or take a day trip together.

Finally, don't spend your life waiting for him to change. Take whatever steps you need to in order to keep you happy and give your children memories, even if he's rarely home. Make home life fun, not a "guilt trip" for him, and he will be more inclined to come home.

It's hard to give to him when he's ignoring you. Pray that God will be your bridegroom, giving you the love and encouragement you need as you walk through this valley, just as Lyndi McCartney once did.

Unplugging His Vine

Sometimes work steals our husbands, and sometimes leisure does, especially those forms of leisure that come in boxes: the TV and the computer. As soon as dinner is over, these husbands retreat into the living room or the den, reemerging only briefly to kiss a child good night. How do you foster a relationship with a husband like this?

Quite simply, it's going to take some work. First, let's look at why they're tuning in so much. Many men have a need for relationship, but they don't know how to express it. Instead, they fill their time so they don't have to deal with it. Other times it's a more mundane answer. The distractions aren't intentional; they're just bad habits. Men may not even particularly want to watch TV or surf the net. They may just be so used to it that it seems like too much effort to do anything else.

Here's where some planning on your part can help. Invite people over for dinner, so you spend time talking (even if it's not just the two of you). People are far less likely to switch on the TV when company's over, and your husband will get used to spending time in relationship.

Start walking after dinner. Every evening at 6:30 I look out my window and see my friends Bill and Heather walking by with their poodle, their two sons, and Heather's parents. They go to the park or around the block, and as they walk, they talk. Explore new hobbies you can do together as a family so that the TV is no longer as attractive. Above all, don't wait for him to switch off and nag him about it; give him a fun alternative. Find family activities he may enjoy—like bowling or mini-golf, or even board games with the family—and he may be less inclined to put down roots in the couch.

Building Temporary Shelter

Once a man realizes one-on-one time is important, you may decide to start regular date nights together. It's a great idea, but don't set your expectations too high. Sometimes aiming for the moon can be intimidating for him. It's expensive, you have to plan the whole evening, and it seems like a lot of work. Then, if the results are less than spectacular, he may not want to repeat it.

Besides, date nights often sound better in theory than they are in practice. My husband and I discovered this last year on Valentine's Day. We dutifully hired a sitter, left the house at 6:00, and went to a lovely restaurant, where we proceeded to have a lovely dinner and a lovely conversation. But we were finished by 7:30, even with the dessert and the coffee. So then what should we do? It was way too early to go home, so we headed, like many other desperate couples, to Chapters (the Canadian equivalent to Barnes and Noble). There we sipped coffee and hot chocolate and leafed through magazines, trying to pretend we were having a romantic time while surreptitiously checking our watches to see when it would be okay to go home.

Chapters eventually closed, so we decided to drive down to a local park by the water and just talk, looking at the stars, before setting the sitter free. Unfortunately, other people in that vicinity had other plans for the night. Soon after we arrived in the parking lot, another car joined us, and a portly man of about sixty stared into our van. At first we were wondering if it was some sort of drug deal he wanted, but he looked a little old. Then he climbed out of his car and walked around to ours, staring at Keith a little funny. Keith roared off in reverse and, defeated, we went home. A while later the police department announced that they had arrested several men for soliciting (and performing) sex acts in that particular park. Romantic escapades are certainly tricky.

Instead of going through contortions to arrange for a perfect evening, take advantage of lower stress alternatives as well. He's more likely to agree, and less likely to run in the opposite direction screaming, if the evening experiences some unexpected twists. Try trading baby-sitting with another couple so that you don't have to pay so much. Maybe even see if that couple will take the children overnight, so you have a whole night uninterrupted. Or just grab what time you do have.

Our daughters are both in kids' club at church on Tuesdays, which runs for an hour and a half. It's not always enough time to grab dinner, but we can often go for dessert or just take a walk together. If you still have young kids at home, see if you can sign them up for activities that will keep them busy simultaneously, so you can grab some time without feeling like you have to make a big production out of it. Another idea is to have lunch with him during the week. Bring a picnic and share twenty minutes together. Or go out for breakfast occasionally. One on one time does not always need to take the entire evening, and he may find it easier to block off time if it doesn't.

As you go through these steps over and over, you'll find you really are building that relationship you crave. You're spending more time together, understanding each other better, and building your family. Eventually you won't just be swinging with him on that jungle vine, but building a new shelter, settling into a closer relationship. You've arrived at the first part of romance: the relationship.

Okay, sisters, here's our chance! We have our tree fort. It's time to decorate, and make it as romantic as we can. How can we make our homes sensuous?

Clearing the Brush

As we saw in chapter 3, little is more stressful than clutter, and stress kills romance. So we need a new attitude about our tree forts— or bedrooms, if you'd rather call them that. Most of us have a habit of sticking things that we want to keep out of sight in the bedroom. The living room becomes the neatest room in the house that's never used, and the bedroom, where we spend the majority of our hours, is crowded and uncomfortable. There's something wrong with this picture. Which room do you consider the most important in the house? Many would say the kitchen, but I disagree. The house is a home because the couple keeps it strong. Where you strengthen your relationship together is the most important room.

Does your bedroom relax and uplift you? If you're going to spend money decorating, this is one of the places to do it. Invest in really comfortable pillows or a decent duvet. An inexpensive paint job on the walls can work wonders by making your bedroom feel bright and comfortable rather than dreary and old. And keep work paraphernalia to a minimum. Your bedroom is the one place where papers, laundry, or books must not pile up. You should not feel guilty in your bedroom.

Finally, your bedroom must be child-free. You simply are not going to feel romantic if a child is sleeping between you, or if you roll over to give your husband a kiss and find an abandoned stuffed bunny between you. And nothing is worse than being in an amorous embrace when a child flings open the door. Invest in a good lock!

Enjoying the Jungle

Now that we've banished distractions from our bedrooms, it's time to awaken the senses. Read Song of Songs, and you will find every sense engaged in romance. She looks beautiful; her eyes are like doves (1:15). The fragrance of her perfume is better than any spice (4:10). His left hand is under her head and his right arm embraces her (2:6). The fragrance of her breath is like apples (7:8). He longs to hear her voice (2:14). Sex does not necessarily engage all the senses every time, but when it's at its best it can. Awakening our senses first, then, increases our capacity for romance.

Touch

Buy bedding and night-clothes that you love. Feeling pampered in our own beds says "romance" to many of us, and it's worth spending the money (especially since lingerie is unlikely to wear out!). Lingerie, though, can be a landmine. My friend Sherry has been married for eighteen years. She told her husband long ago, "I will wear sexy, pretty lingerie, but I will not dress like a prostitute. I will look pretty, not slutty." And she has still managed to find plenty of silky garments that meet her requirements that they both enjoy touching! If lingerie is a landmine for other reasons—namely the shape of the body you're trying to squeeze into it—don't worry. We'll talk about this more in the next chapter.

A bath together also gets your body warm and ready for embraces. When it's time for these embraces, make sure that you spend time just touching to "awaken love," as the lovers do in Song of Songs. If he wants to hurry through this process, slow him down. Touch, after all, is actually necessary for most women to achieve orgasm. The vagina has very few nerve endings compared to the clitoris, so in order to get aroused, most women need this time of pure attention to our bodies.

Taste

Do chocolates help you to feel more sensuous? Strawberries? Whatever it is, have some on hand. He'll soon learn that if you draw out the seduction part of the evening, the whole evening is more enjoyable!

One thing my husband and I often do is plan for a lovely dinner after the children have gone to bed. I'll fix them something simple (they're more likely to eat that anyway), and I save "the yucky green stuff" for when Mommy and Daddy are alone. After a leisurely, candlelit meal, we feel grateful for each other and more inclined to show it.

Smell

With so many scented candles available now, it's easy to make your bedroom smell like a welcoming oasis. Perhaps you won't be perfumed in myrrh, as Solomon was, but you can wear perfume if your husband likes it.

One of the big turn-offs, though, is if rather than being perfumed with myrrh he's perfumed with eau de sweat. Or if his kisses, instead of tasting like honey, taste like the Caesar salad dressing with extra garlic he ate earlier. Unfortunately, this can be a very delicate subject because no one wants to insult somebody's lack of personal hygiene. Yet as wonderful as natural pheromones are purported to smell, I firmly believe few things smell better than soap. My friend Sherry uses this technique to deal with the sticky problem: She walks into the bedroom wearing that pretty lingerie we talked about and says sweetly, "I've had my shower, and I'm all yours. Now how about you?" Her husband is usually done with that shower pretty quickly. If this is a common problem, try making it your evening routine to shower and brush your teeth together. You'll both feel fresh, and you will have had some time engaging other senses, too.

Sound

In *Great Sexpectations,* Robert and Rosemary Barnes recount the story of a woman who was always waiting for her husband to be romantic.[2] One of the things she enjoyed was soft music, and even though she told him, he never seemed to remember. Then one day she realized she could turn on the CD player as well as he could. When she stopped waiting for him to remember her preference, and resenting him when he didn't, she was able to relax and enjoy their time together.

Sound can also be awakened by talking together and sharing what you love about each other. Certainly tell him why you love him, but don't be afraid to awaken other senses by telling him what you find sexy—his hands, his shoulders, his chest. Whisper what you want to do to him, or what you'd like him to do to you, and you turn up the sparks!

Sight

Finally we come to sight. A soft glow from candles is much more forgiving than strong lights and lets you see enough to look into each other's eyes and enjoy the experience together. Sight is also important for his arousal. If you, however, are scared of any light that may reveal the flawed body on the bed, keep reading. Chapter 8 is especially for you!

Asking Him to Help

Once you've figured out what you need to feel romantic, let your husband in on the secret. You can even write it out for him, calling it "20 Ways to Light My Fire." Now he has something tangible to make seduction easier. You may wish he instinctively knew, but isn't it better if you give him some clues so your dreams have a greater likelihood of coming true? Maybe running the bath for you while he puts the kids in bed would be number one on your list. Or maybe it's something easier, like turning on that CD, washing some strawberries, or bringing home some chocolates. Tell him what makes you tick, and he's more likely to become your knight in shining armor.

For Him

Why is buying something as predictable as flowers romantic? As silly as it seems, to women it means a great deal. It means you made the effort to care about her feelings.

Without taking the emotional into account when it comes to sex, you could be making love to anybody. She needs you to make the effort to show her that she matters as a person. That's what romance is, and it can be divided into two different areas: building the relationship, and building the outside trappings that show that sex is more than just physical.

First, she really needs a relationship with you. She wants to spend time talking together and doing things together. Providing for the family is important, but most women would trade some money for more time with their husbands. Don't work all weekend. Try every now and then, out of the blue, to surprise her with a date night.

Now it's time to make sex involve all the senses to show that it's not just about your genitals. In the Song of Songs, Solomon and the Shunammite enjoy every sense. Sex incorporates all of who you are. What can stimulate her sense of touch? Taste? Sound? Buy her some chocolates, some nice bedding, or some pretty (not slutty!) lingerie. And you know something? You need to smell nice, too. That means taking a shower before you come to bed if you've had a busy day, and it definitely means brushing your teeth. Awaken the senses, and you'll experience sex on a new level.

Chapter 7

Who Wears the Pants in This Family?

A few years ago my husband and I took ballroom dancing classes. We learned to waltz, fox-trot, and cha-cha, but most of all we learned that things work better when I remember he's the man.

As my husband and I laughed, stepped on each others' toes, and watched other couples help each other up off the floor, a new kind of bond grew between us. You see, ballroom dancing only works when the dancers accept that they are very different. If you both try to do the same thing, you *will* look stupid and you *will* fall. It's that simple. But when you accept your role, a beautiful rhythm is found that is so much more graceful than anything you could do individually. As you find that rhythm, something very romantic happens. I can almost guarantee that romance followed all those couples home every night; in fact, I think that's why all the men, despite the toppling, wore those silly grins on their faces. They knew what was coming.

Ballroom dancing is experiencing unprecedented growth right now, to the point that it may soon be named an Olympic sport. It's not hard to see why. In this world where men can do anything women can do, and women can do anything men can do, it's very comforting to do something that reminds us that we are not interchangeable.

What Is Gender?

Sex, for it to work best, requires this perspective, too. Because sex is the joining of one man with one woman, the very act reinforces that we are not the same. And if we're not comfortable with this fact, then we're going to find it harder to enjoy making love. Unfortunately, our culture is attacking this traditional idea of "men" and "women," threatening our sexual relationships. Let's look at why gender identities are important, and how they're being attacked, to get a better idea of how we can keep our sexual relationships healthy in this culture.

Let's turn first to the nature of gender. Leanne Payne, who has written a number of books about the importance of a proper gender identity, says masculinity is "the power to honor the truth—to speak it and *be* it."[1] Femininity, on the other hand, is the desire and ability to respond to truth. Elisabeth Elliott defined them in similar terms, saying that masculinity at heart is initiation, while femininity is response.[2] This mirrors the sexual act and probably explains why God made us to join together in this way.

These categories, though, aren't absolutes. This doesn't mean women can't make decisions or that men can't be nurturing! In fact, we all need both masculine and feminine characteristics so that we can respond appropriately in relationships, but also so that we can act decisively when we need to. Besides, as C. S. Lewis said, compared to God we are all feminine.[3] God Himself is transcendent, and has elements of both genders. All of us, too, will have both masculine and feminine characteristics within us. To enjoy sex, though—or even more fundamentally, to feel comfortable in our own skin—we have to embrace the gender God has given us.

Why We Need Gender

How does failing to feel comfortable as a man or a woman affect our relationships? At its most extreme, people may be tempted toward homosexuality.[4] But that's not the most common problem. When we can't accept ourselves in our gender, we can't accept our sexuality. For this complementary arrangement to work, women must be able to trust, and men must be trustworthy and able to initiate. You must be vulnerable; he must protect. As the Song of Songs says, "His banner over me is love" (2:4). The cultural and familial forces that tradition-ally affirmed these traits, though, are rapidly disappearing. Of course, this is not without its advantages. Women are no longer completely dependent on men. We can pursue our dreams and, if necessary, pro-tect ourselves. Men can express their feelings. In other words, we both are free to express the "other." What we are not as free to do today is to express the primary characteristics that we need in order to meet together sexually. Let's see why.

The Disappearance of Dads

Psychologists tell us that it's the father who actually affirms our gender identities. The mother cannot make the son comfortable in his manhood, or the daughter in her womanhood.[5] Yet this generation is the story of the failure of fathers. Though many are wonderful, far too many are not, and the whole society is reeling from their negligence. These absent dads—whether absent physically or emotionally—leave their children with only mothers to guide them. Their sons suffer the most, because the daughter at least has Mom to emulate. Boys are left with no one to tell him what it means to be a man.

When masculinity is not properly affirmed, it becomes perverted, usually in one of two ways: either as a drive for power, or as passivity. The Middle East is an example of the hypermasculine gone awry: suicide bombers deny truth and creation all in one breath. In Western society, too often we see the other extreme: passivity, where men fail to live up to commitments, and throw their lives away in front of the TV, all because they are unable to honor what is most important. It's hard to have a healthy sexual relationship with either extreme, be-cause ultimately he doesn't know what being male means.

If you're married to someone who has not been affirmed, you can-not do it for him. He needs a father. But even if his earthly one isn't willing or able, his heavenly One is. Encourage him to find masculine friends to talk with, and to explore the Bible to see how God sees him as a man.

The Cultural Attack on Gender

Our gender identities are not eroding just because families are failing, though; the culture is also changing. When the Titanic sank in 1912, some of the richest men in the world helped women and children they didn't even know into lifeboats, and then stood back as the ship went down. They willingly went to their deaths because their honor demanded it. Women and children first; men last. Everybody knew that, and everybody did it.

Yet when James Cameron made his epic movie about the disaster a few years ago, he portrayed the scene very differently, showing people clamoring to get a seat in the precious boats. Today, the idea of a man giving up his seat to save a woman is nonsense. Nobody would have believed how it happened. It's so far out of our consciousness that Cameron couldn't even portray it.

Why was it different in 1912? In those days, people had a strong sense of what it meant to be a man or a woman. Women were to be treated well. They were the mothers, and children needed their mothers. A father's job was to protect those women and children at all cost.

Today if you believe this you're labeled "sexist." We have even pushed to ensure that women can serve side by side with men in the military. As a country, we allow single mothers to fight for the lives of able-bodied men. What a reversal! I don't mean to argue the merits of women in the military, though many have written eloquently on the subject.[6] I mean only to say that the idea that women constitute a special class of person, solely because of their gender, has completely evaporated.

This isn't men's fault, either. Women have been the most vocal in saying that we don't need men. Do you remember Gloria Steinem's famous quote: "A woman without a man is like a fish without a bicycle"? Though this is how Steinem may have seen the world, she was wrong. Deep down, women still yearn for white knights. In our world, salmon have training wheels. And this is only natural. God is the synthesis of both male and female; He placed inside each of us a desire for that same synthesis, which is best achieved through marriage.

The 9/11 attack was a huge shock to our system and allowed some of our latent common sense to resurface. Our heroes were the firemen, the police, and the passengers who fought back on flight 187, almost all of whom were male and able to do what they had to do because of their strength. Donald Rumsfeld, though over seventy, became a kind of sex symbol because he talked like a man. Instead of echoing Clinton—"I feel your pain"—he was far more likely to want to inflict pain, and lots of it, on the bad guys, and he wasn't afraid to say so.

The Attack on Little Boys

It took a disaster to let common sense shine again, but I'm afraid this cultural trend won't be sustained because there's too much moving in the other direction. Everything is increasingly being feminized, and masculinity is under attack. Let me talk about schools for a moment, because this is especially dangerous and evident here. Schools tend to emphasize feminine traits like teamwork, encourage children to talk about feelings, and try to avoid too much competition. Many even have "student of the week" awards to reward kids who have been nice to others, rather than to reward those who have made the biggest improvement in math.

Schools concentrate far less on teaching facts—like multiplication tables, dates of historical events, and spelling—than they do on teaching opinions and supporting students' feelings. One man in Britain wrote about how we're even changing our curriculum to mirror girls' concerns.

Whereas before a typical history question might have read "Give an account of the key events during the reign of Queen Victoria, and explain why they are significant," the question now reads, "Describe what it might have been like growing up in a Manchester poor house during the reign of Queen Victoria." Instead of fact-retention and recall, in which girls and boys are roughly equally proficient, the question now requires empathy, something that females excel in, and at which males are useless.[7]

If we hold up feminine traits as the ideal, at some level we're telling boys they're not good enough. Besides, many masculine traits are also very useful in learning. Studies show that boys tend to value independence, competition, and success, and all students could benefit from an injection of these values. Instead of viewing each value as useful in its place, though, we're trying to teach boys to be more like girls.

And it's not just what they study in school. Many schools' zero-tolerance violence policies have meant that boys can no longer wrestle at recess or even play tag. The roughhousing that boys tend to like to do is now outlawed. Boys cannot be boys. And the result? Boys are failing at higher rates than girls; they now make up a minority on college campuses; they're rarely on the honor rolls. This attempt to mold boys into girls' shoes is failing, but few seem prepared to understand the root cause: boys and girls are different, and that's okay.

The Attack on Big Boys

This assault on gender identities isn't confined to the schools. In the workplace, too, more emphasis is being placed on teambuilding, which can be beneficial, but nonetheless is elevating typically feminine traits. "Multilateralism," wherein we respond and consult with each other, is considered superior to "unilateralism," wherein we act alone according to our values, even if those values are true and right.

And what about fashion? Everything is becoming more androgynous. The biggest new sexual identity group is transsexuals or bisexuals, people who want to dress like the opposite sex or who want to have sex with either sex. Howard Dean, when running for the 2004 Democratic presidential nomination, famously declared he was a "metrosexual," a heterosexual accepting of every other sexual identity and very in touch with his feminine side.[8] A Broadway play about Boy George, the 1980s transvestite, produced by Rosie O'Donnell, had a short, bur well-publicized run on Broadway. And in a move that makes me shake my head, Wesleyan University in Connecticut has decided to offer a "gender-blind" dormitory, where people who aren't sure of their gender identity can room with others who aren't sure of their gender identity, regardless of their biological sex.[9]

What This Means for Men

All the ways that men formerly used to define themselves have slowly been stripped away, and now they're told that their most basic instincts are somehow wrong. They're not supposed to be aggressive; they're supposed to want to empathize with everyone; they're not supposed to see women as sex objects, even when their own hormones are raging and these women are wearing pants down around their hips.

When we deny men the ability to figure out who they truly are, it's hard for a man to know how to act in a marriage. Does he order her around? Does he let her take command? When they're not given proper role models to channel their natural inclinations, men can rebel in opposite directions.

What This Means for Women

When men aren't comfortable being men, it's hard for women, too. Who is our protector? Who will be the strong one we can rely on? Something precious is stolen from us when godly masculinity is silenced. But not only do we miss our own better half, we also lose our own identity. Even though much of society is being "feminized," this isn't necessarily a triumph for women. Femininity has been expanded to every aspect of society: everything is feminine now, so what's special about it?

I'm not arguing for a return to the 1950s, when girls were girls and men were men, as Archie Bunker used to sing in *All in the Family.* Plenty of problems for married couples existed then, too. Yet we do need to find ways to love the fact that we are, indeed, women married to actual men.

Reclaiming Your Femininity

Can we reverse these trends that attack gender? And do we even want to? Many of us can't return to the traditional family where the husband is the only one working, and we certainly don't want him to stop vacuuming or bathing the kids. Nor should we have to! Instead, we need to separate the cultural attack on femininity from the new tasks that we do. We don't have to become human doormats; we do have to understand that God made us male and female for a purpose.

Pampering Yourself

Can we revel in the fact that we're women? Let's look at some of the things that help us feel feminine, and see how we can encourage them, whatever our job situation. It may seem silly, but I think top of this list is concern over appearance. After all, God made men to be visual, and one of the ways that we women can enjoy being women is to enjoy the way we look (as long as we're not trying to entice other men!).[10] Men don't take this same care with their appearance. Whenever our family gives in to pressure and succumbs to the torture better known as the trip to the department store portrait studio, I'm always amazed that it takes me an hour to transform myself, and my husband can declare himself ready in three minutes flat, looking exactly the same as he always does.

After we've been talking about work roles and money, it may sound superficial to suggest we value our physical appearance. But the physical is important, especially when it comes to sex. After all, the physical is the one area in our lives where we have to be either masculine or feminine. When we take care to feel feminine, we've taken a huge step ahead in our sex lives, even if it doesn't seem in vogue to say so.

Interestingly, I think advertisers understand the unconscious desire of women to feel pretty, better than we do. If you peruse the cosmetics ads at the beginning of women's magazines, at least half the time the woman will be staring off into space. She is being watched. Ads for men's products, instead, show them staring straight into the camera, as if issuing a challenge.

I don't mean we should turn ourselves into teenage sex objects, and I know that for many of us, our feelings about our bodies are one of the biggest stumbling blocks to a healthy sex life. But taking an interest in your appearance can give you sexual confidence, because you're remembering who you are.

There's also no need to become what he thinks is pretty. Some men, like my husband, have a preference for women in long hair. Keith, however, is oblivious to all the mousse and blow drying that would be involved in making my long hair do anything other than hang there limply. I think it's difficult for most women over thirty to pull off long hair with panache. Cut my hair and highlight it and I look much more sophisticated, and I feel far less frumpy!

You don't have to become what society says is feminine, either. Maybe you'll never be a make-up kind of person, and maybe you hate skirts. The important thing is not to be an image of someone else, but to take care in being yourself. Buy clothes that you feel good in, get a nice haircut, or pamper yourself with a bubble bath. As you feel comfortable in your skin, you'll feel ready to invite him in!

Wave the White Flag

Now that we've dealt with the physical, let's look at some of those relationship patterns that we can change so that we can feel like women. First, let's surrender the war. I've been a soldier in it, and it's not fun. If you're not sure what war I'm talking about, you're lucky. It means you haven't been faced with the indoctrination on campuses today and in corporate boardrooms or the media. But the war is real, even though it didn't start out as a war. When Susan B. Anthony first pushed for women's rights, she did so using the Bible and embracing woman's special roles as wife and mother rather than rejecting them. Many Christians forget that the feminist movement has not historically been anti-family; on the contrary, the first feminists said some of the most eloquent things ever said to defend the Christian faith and the Christian family.

Yet in the 1960s a new group of feminists emerged who fanned the flames of the current war. The feminist movement was no longer a fight for justice and human dignity, but instead it became a fight between the sexes, where one side must lose. It was an attack on marriage, motherhood, and everything feminine, perhaps made most infamous by Susan Brownmiller's thesis that "all sex is rape."

Girls are now taught that they must be wary of men in order to guard their rights. It sets up a false battle line between women and men. Yet Christ came to break down walls, not to build them up. Love, remember, keeps no record of wrongs. We should look at the individual, as God does, rather than judging a whole class of people, as modern feminists tend to.

Becoming One

It's not enough just to feel confident and comfortable as women; we also need to feel comfortable as wives. If you're going to have a fulfilling marriage and a satisfying sex life, you have to become one, with your husband the male half and you the female half. However, a number of factors can render this kind of "oneness" a distant dream. Many of us desire to remain independent, even when we're married, because we're used to doing things our own way. We don't want to be joined as much as we want to continue doing what we've always done, with him alongside for the ride. As the average age of first marriage increases, couples find that integrating two very distinct lives can pose quite a challenge.[11] Other problems are more complex, especially the fear of trusting a man when we've been abused in the past. No matter how much we may love our husbands, it's difficult to place our lives, let alone our bodies, in our husbands' hands.

Yet many women are encountering a far more mundane cause of this lack of mutuality. As William Bennett points out in *The Broken Hearth*, the ability to support oneself financially, despite its many positive aspects, is still a two-edged sword for women.[12] The contract that says he will support and protect you isn't necessary anymore. It's easier for a marriage to split up, and this makes it more likely that one has to maintain at least a slight distance to protect oneself in case the marriage does end. In so doing, it's easy to erode some of the relationship traits that make sex great. We no longer have to trust him as we once did, even though the ability to completely give ourselves is integral to the sexual act. Simply because of anatomy, we are the recipients. For many women, that now feels wrong, and even unnatural. So what do we do? We maintain separate bank accounts. We keep track of who earns what or who pays for what. We aren't one.

The hurdles to mutuality don't stop there, either. A common theme from contemporary women's writings is that women are so tired from working all day that they just don't want to have sex when they get home.[13] And when women work, most men work harder, too, leaving the whole family more stressed and tired. Here's what Dr. Jane Greer, the online sex therapist for *Redbook* magazine, said in an interview with Caitlyn Flanagan:

> "Marriage has changed, . . . In the old days the husband was the breadwinner. The wife had the expectation of raising the children and pleasing him. Now they're both working and both taking care of the children, and they're too exhausted and resentful to have sex." I asked Greer the obvious question: If a couple is not having sex because of job pressures and one partner quits working, does the couple have more sex? The answer was immediate and unequivocal: *"Absolutely!"*[14]

A new best-selling novel has a similar theme: Kate Reddy, the heroine from Allison Pearson's *I Don't Know How She Does It,* has a horrible sex life until, at the end of the book, she quits her job and comes home. Counselors have even created a new category called "the sex-starved marriage,"[15] largely filled by couples who both work.

Exhaustion certainly plays a part in the lack of desire these couples may feel. But I think psychologically there's more to it than that. If you're both working, whether or not he does his share of the work to keep the house going becomes a much more stressful subject. It's easy for resentment to build up. As children age, too, often parents' schedules outside of work revolve so much around the kids that there's little left for couplehood. Parenthood, not your relationship, begins defining your life.

None of these things are automatic outcomes in a dual-income family, and if you both work there's no reason that a healthy sex life and a healthy marriage aren't possible. It may just mean more intense negotiation on handling the workload at home, and more care that children do not hijack a marriage. When there's less time to go around, these things all pose greater threats.

I would also encourage you to make sure that both of you are working for the right reasons. If you can survive on one income, or if both of you can work fewer hours, consider it. Life is stressful enough, and we need to consider where God wants us to spend our time. For many of us, that will involve a career, but some, I fear, work because that's what we're "supposed" to do, not because we feel a calling. Don't live life on the default setting; think critically about where you want your life to go. Paid work takes up so much time and energy. Let's be sure before either of us leaves the house that it is necessary and that it's where God wants us to be.

Finally, let's recognize how marriage can actually benefit us when we do let go of our need to maintain independence. Linda Waite and Maggie Gallagher, in their groundbreaking book *The Case for Marriage,* argue that one of the benefits of being married is specialization: you do what's easiest for you, and he does what's easiest for him.[16] In the end, you have a nicer home, a bigger paycheck, and more well adjusted children. If you divide everything 50/50, you'll lose this benefit, because you'll be doing some things that he would be better at, and he'll be doing some that you would do better. (In our house, that's the laundry. I have plenty of wrecked delicates to prove it, and my husband is now banished from the laundry room forever.) As we recognize our gifts, our family blooms. We discover we need each other, and we start to trust each other accordingly. When you're able to trust and relinquish some pride, you'll find the family you raise is happier, healthier, and much more cohesive. And so is your marriage.

Supporting His Masculinity

Our own femininity is often reinforced in opposition to his masculinity. It's the "otherness" that is attractive. If we want to feel feminine, then, we can look feminine, we can act feminine, and we can support him as he acts masculine.

So let him be a guy. That doesn't mean inviting all his friends over to smoke cigars and play poker every night, but it does mean not nagging him to tell you how he feels (he probably doesn't know) or expecting him to act like your best friend would.

What does he like to do that's typically masculine? Does he like to fix cars, to hunt, to play strategy games, or to take a computer apart? Does he like to be in charge of committees, or be a vocal spokesperson for an important community initiative? Instead of viewing these things as attacks on your marriage, support him in them. Talk to him frankly, of course, about how you can negotiate a balance so that he doesn't neglect the family, but let him be a man.

That also means allowing him to parent his way. Maybe he wrestles with your son instead of kissing him. My husband reacted totally differently to being a dad than I did to being a mom. He wanted to play with Rebecca, bouncing her in the air in such a way that I almost fainted. I, instead, cuddled her close to me. But she needs both of us, and when we tear our kids away from our husbands because they're not doing it "right," we criticize their masculinity and we undermine their parenting skills.

If you let him act like a man, he's more likely to feel comfortable with who he is, and his ability to enjoy sex and to perform sexually is going to be greatly enhanced. But so is yours. The more you can see him as something different from you, someone you can find mysterious and exciting, the more feminine you will feel. Let the music begin!

For Him

Guys today are under attack. Perhaps you've always felt that, but it's hard to admit it because all the politically correct forces try to tell you that it's not true. But look at schools, at the workplace, or at the media, and you'll find that typically masculine traits are being undermined in favor of typically feminine traits. The pendulum has swung the other way, and we need to wait a little for it to swing back (read p. 115 about the situation in schools, if you want an example).

And here's the problem: sex requires both a man and a woman. If you're not comfortable with your masculinity, or if she's not comfortable with her femininity, then you're going to have a hard time relating to each other sexually. I'm not talking about either of you flirting with homosexuality; I'm talking about the normal problems that occur when we forget that men and women are different and stop cherishing those differences. It's those differences that are sexy.

What is masculinity? It's the power to do and speak the truth, to take initiative, and to stand up for what's right. I've told her that she should encourage you when you do some typically guy things. To help your masculinity yourself, make sure you have some male friends. You may also have trouble living out masculinity if you didn't have a good father figure to affirm it in you. Seek out a mentor to pray and study with so you can understand how God loves you and how He uniquely equips you to act in the world. Finally, encourage her in her femininity. Compliment her when she looks particularly pretty. Take ballroom dancing lessons. Do whatever it takes to remember that you're a man and she's a woman. That's a recipe for more excitement in a marriage.

Chapter 8

Mirror, Mirror on the Wall

We cannot complete a book on sex without dealing with one of the "biggest" obstacles to our libido: catching a glimpse of ourselves in the mirror.

Leslie knows how humbling that can be. A gym teacher for most of her adult life, she was active, working out every day. Then she moved, switched jobs, and a few months later looked down to find a tire around her waist. Her sex drive plummeted. She was so embarrassed that she found it difficult even to think about sex. All she wanted to do was pull the covers up over her head.

While commiserating with a friend one day, she heard an even worse story. This woman, who had nursed four children, was on a much-needed seaside vacation. But as she lay down on her back to sunbathe, to her horror she found that her breasts, rather than sitting up, had lobbed over under each armpit. They didn't just migrate south; they migrated east and west as well.

We women are notoriously critical of our bodies. Almost all of us can name something about our bodies we don't like (I can name five without even pausing for breath), and usually this relates to our weight. This doesn't even necessarily correspond to what our bodies actually look like. Those who are ten pounds overweight can feel just as abysmal about themselves as those who are fifty pounds overweight. Anorexics who are life-threateningly thin still feel fat. We have an image in our heads of what we should look like, and we punish ourselves if we don't think we meet it.

When we don't measure up to those expectations, feeling comfortable enough in our bodies to want to make love seems very difficult. An American Health for Women survey found that 23 percent of women felt too fat for sex, and, not surprisingly, they suffered from low desire levels. One of the reasons we women are so conscious of our appearance is that traditionally this is how women attracted men, who would then be their benefactors. A larger number of women in the workplace may have erased some of the need for this support, but the cultural significance of women's appearance hasn't waned. Even today, there's much more variety in what movies' leading men look like (and especially in how old they are) than there is in how the leading women appear.

It's hardly surprising, then, that little makes us feel as guilty as being unable to lose weight. Yet because we feel this guilt, it is no longer simply an appearance issue. It's easy to believe excess weight means we have no self-control, which is actually a character issue. We don't just lose confidence physically; our self-image is threatened, making loving and respecting ourselves, something necessary for any healthy sex life, increasingly remote. We buy into society's values, and in the process we rob ourselves of peace of mind, confidence, and even our sexuality.

When Guilt Weighs You Down

This insight is sadly lacking even among my friends. A few months ago, sitting around the table at a Wendy's restaurant, one could almost taste the guilt. The five of us sat sullenly, picking over our french fries and comparing our "weight issues."

"I try to exercise, but I'm just so busy," lamented Esther. "I know I have to try harder."

The others all agreed. The reason they were too heavy must be because they were too lazy. They had all been on diets before, but the weight had never stayed off. They had no "self-control." As I glanced around the table, I found that hard to believe. These women were the lifeblood of our community, serving in their families, at their workplaces, and in the church. Yet there they sat, depressed and defeated, because they could not stay thin.

Heather of Waco, Texas, knows exactly how they feel. After battling a food addiction all her life, she joined Weigh Down, a well-known, but now largely discredited Christian weight loss group, and accepted Christ.[1] Yet her newfound joy didn't last. The leader preached that if she relied on God, she wouldn't need to turn to food. "Whenever I ate," Heather says, "I felt guilty, like I had rejected God." Even after losing more than one hundred pounds, Heather still felt a wall between her and God. "I couldn't approach Him with the extra weight I still had. It was proof that I was a sinner."

For many Christian women like Heather, weight gain is no longer just a health issue. It's a spiritual battle they are waging—and all too often losing. The alarming increase in obesity certainly constitutes a serious health crisis that needs to be addressed. To live out God's purposes for our lives, we need to be as healthy as we can. And we all have more energy when our bodies are in great shape. But when we focus solely on the obesity crisis, we sometimes ignore the spiritual crisis that is also occurring.

Heather felt she couldn't read the Bible without hearing how God condemned her. My friends felt that they lacked many fruits of the Spirit. These women dealt with guilt of varying degrees of severity, but they all suffered from the same problem: feeling that they were failing God because they could not control their weight, and feeling low self worth because of it. How can we enjoy fun, intimate relationships with our husbands if we don't feel worthy of God's acceptance?

Over the last few years, many Christian leaders have been challenging our whole approach to weight loss, partly in reaction to harmful Christian teaching and partly due to new research that shows how complex weight loss is. Best-selling author Liz Curtis Higgs once started a weight loss group. Then she began questioning the values involved in weight loss, and she wrote *"One Size Fits All" and Other Fables* to free women from the guilt of weight gain.[2] Neva Coyle, author of the phenomenal best-seller *Free to Be Thin*, regained one hundred pounds and now encourages women to focus on their relationship to Jesus and not to food. And across the country, Christian health professionals are encouraging us to take another look at our motivations and methods of losing weight. Let's take a "weight reality check" and examine some of the faulty premises we may cling to as we punish ourselves—and inadvertently our husbands—for not living up to society's unrealistic demands.

Premise 1: "It's All My Fault I'm Heavy"

At first glance, it seems impossible to refute this premise. After all, we all know we gain weight because we eat too much and don't exercise enough. We'd love to pass the blame to someone else, but how can we? No one forced us to eat those cakes or pies. Studying historical weight trends, though, shows it's not as straightforward as we may think. According to a recent Harris poll, more than 80 percent of us who are over twenty-five are overweight, a rate that has increased 61 percent over the last decade alone.[3] With numbers like these, our weight problems can't be simple personal failures.

A far more logical explanation is that our society has set up the conditions for us to gain weight. Fifty years ago, if we five women had been having the same conversation, we would not have been sitting in a fast food restaurant. We would have been in someone's house, having coffee and sandwiches. Instead of five vans in the driveway there may have been one car and a bunch of strollers, since most of us would have walked. And instead of four of the five of us being heavy, probably only two of us would have been. Our lives are completely different today. We drive to work, we sit at desks, and we watch TV, at the same time that junk food is so readily available.

Christian nutritionist Pam Smith, author of *The SMART Weigh: A 5-point Plan for Losing Weight Without Losing Your Soul,* says that "our bodies were masterfully designed to survive—and thrive."[4] The way they do this, though, is by stockpiling energy in the form of fat to protect against times of famine and sickness. Unfortunately, we no longer need them to! But it gets worse. Our bodies often interpret stresses, like deadlines and teenagers, as famine. So they store fat even when we're not overeating!

These lifestyle issues, however, don't necessarily affect everyone the same way. My friend Rosemary works out four days a week at a health club and bikes all over town, but she still carries an extra twenty pounds. She's in better shape than anyone else in the aerobics class, but you wouldn't guess it by looking at her. Her body is simply too efficient at making fat. In many important areas of life, people today aren't accepting enough personal responsibility. This is one where perhaps we're accepting too much.

Premise 2: "I'm Letting God Down When I Don't Lose Weight"

Although most obesity is probably caused by our lifestyles or our genetic traits, some women no doubt do use food improperly, perhaps by turning to it for comfort, just as Heather did. However, even in these cases, is it appropriate to feel such spiritual condemnation? We all struggle with sin. Even Paul said, "What I want to do I do not do, but what I hate I do" (Rom. 7:15). Struggles will be a part of our lives on this side of heaven. This struggle may be more difficult to live with than others because it's so visible, like wearing a neon sign advertising the fact that we're not perfect. Yet just because we struggle—and often fail—does not mean we've lost God's approval. Remember, this is the God who said, "There is now no condemnation for those who are in Christ Jesus" (Rom. 8:1).

Premise 3: "I Can't Feel Good About Myself if I'm Big"

When we can't accept ourselves, we forget something very important: God felt we were precious enough to die for. He doesn't say, "I'll only love you if you're a size 8." He simply says, "I love you." We don't need to become something He can be proud of; instead, the value we have in His eyes is only because He made us and redeemed us.

God certainly wants us to strive to be the best we can, but that will never affect His love or acceptance of us, and so it shouldn't affect our own, either. We can't feel other people's love and acceptance, including our husband's, if we don't feel God's. If God doesn't love us, then we are truly unlovable. So remind yourself that your failures—even imagined ones—never stop God from loving you. The father ran to the prodigal son when he saw him in the distance, and that's what God does to us, too. He doesn't wait for you to come to Him, already perfect. He runs to embrace you. He loves you. That is an objective fact that cannot change. Ask God to let you feel Him put His arms around you, and you may soon feel more welcoming of others' arms, as well!

Premise 4: "But I Need to Be Attractive!"

For many of us, losing weight has little to do with health and everything to do with appearance. Why else would so many people choose obviously unhealthy ways to lose weight, like fasting, purging, or eating only grapefruit (blech!).

The Bible never describes what the ideal Christian woman looks like. Instead, God says: "Man looks at the outward appearance, but the LORD looks at the heart" (1 Sam. 16:7). If physical attractiveness is not high on His priority list, perhaps it's time to rethink ours. Besides, our idea of physical attractiveness isn't even on a sliding scale. We so value thinness that a size 12 won't do, even if a woman has already lost fifty pounds. We are building a cage for ourselves as we try to squeeze into this mold, and in so doing we're rejecting the bodies we have. If we do that, how can we see them as sources of pleasure for us or for our husbands? We need to unlock that cage.

Embracing Your Body

Rejecting Guilt

If you're going to live a life free of guilt, it's time to get rid of all those trappings of guilt. How many different sizes of clothes are in your closet? If you do not fit most of your clothes, then you may as well put a sign up in your bedroom declaring, "You're *fat!* You're *fat!*"

Every time you open your closet, or peek in a drawer, you're confronted with your failure to fit into all those dresses and slacks that once looked so good on you. You're not focusing on who you are now; you're still focusing on who you think you should be.

If you don't want to get rid of them because they're so beautiful, or so expensive, or even so meaningful, ask yourself this: are they worth all the room they take up? Are they worth reminding yourself, day in and day out, that you're heavier than you once were? Why not use those clothes to make yourself feel happy instead? Surely there's a single mother you know who may not have money to buy herself some great clothes. Give them to her. Or maybe you should just give them all to charity. Then, if you ever do lose weight, think of the fun you'll have buying a new wardrobe!

Expressing Yourself Physically

Sometimes when we feel unattractive we project that same feeling to others. We buy nondescript clothes, because we don't want to draw attention to ourselves. We drape ourselves in clothes that make us look awful because we think, at some level, that that is who we are. But Jesus doesn't care about how you look; He cares about your heart. You are accepted. You are free. You are loved.

There is no reason for you to feel terrible in your clothes. Anyone, no matter what her body type, can find clothes that make her feel wonderful and reflect who she is. If you are extroverted, buy some bright, dramatic clothes. If you're a wise listener, a helpful comforter, buy some soft, feminine clothes that reflect that. Let what you wear be an extension of who you are, and not an attempt to hide or, even worse, to punish yourself. If you're not sure what's so unique about you or how to express it, find some girlfriends and go shopping! Let them help you choose a few outfits that suit you. It's better to have six outfits that you feel great in than thirty that make you feel ugly. The clothes don't need to be expensive, either; they just need to make you feel happy. This isn't being shallow; it's just an acknowledgment that as women, clothes have the ability to affect our emotions.

We tend to think that when we're naked we're the most real. Yet I don't think that's true. When we shed our clothes, we become male and female.[5] When we're clothed, though, we can express our individuality. I don't think this is a vain pursuit. I think it's celebrating the people God made us to be.

Many of us don't know who we are, and that's why we have such trouble in clothes shops (others of us have trouble because we don't fit a particular size, but that's another problem!). When I'm able to feel more like Sheila in my clothes, I'm more able to feel like Sheila when I'm shedding them with my husband. I have something authentic to share.

Uncovering Your Beauty

You may be thinking, *Great, I have the clothes, but if I'm going to have sex I have to take them* off, *and that's what I'm afraid of!* You know God accepts you, but what about your husband? And what about you?

Here's some encouragement: every pretty person that you see most likely looks worse naked than you think. Very few people look better naked than they do clothed. There just aren't that many perfect figures, and the ones that we think of as perfect are probably unnatural anyway. I once read that Barbie, if she were human, would be 44-12-21. She wouldn't even be able to stand up! I think the biggest enemy of a healthy body image, and a healthy sex life, isn't actually the mirror revealing all our flaws. It's instead (here we go again!) the television screen, which promotes something that for most of us isn't even possible, even with all the dieting and exercise in the world. If we want to feel better about ourselves, one of the best things we can do is to switch it off.

Looking good is largely a function of exuding confidence; it is not an objective measurement of body parts. That's why the Bible says a woman's beauty is her spirit. It isn't an attempt to be trite; it's true. Think about the women you think look fabulous. Is it their figures or the way they carry themselves? Now think of the women you do know with good figures. Are they necessarily what you would call pretty? Many are not. Beauty does not come from having a perfect body. Beauty truly bubbles up from within, and when we cultivate our characters, allowing ourselves to live a life of abundance and reveling in the grace that God has given us, we will be beautiful.

Treating Your Body Well

If we should not aim to lose weight to feel good about ourselves, to be beautiful, or to feel closer to God, then should we worry about weight at all? The answer to this involves changing how we view our bodies: let's see them not as a source of our self-worth, but as the vehicle through which we can fulfill God's purposes for our lives. It is, after all, easier to serve Him if we're healthy, rested, and have lots of energy than if we're lethargic and sick.

My mother's weight slowly crept up over fifteen years, and finally she decided to do something about it. Though she has never been an athletic person, she started exercising for forty minutes every morning. In the summer months, she takes her exercise machine out on her deck and exercises watching the birds at the feeders and the squirrels collecting nuts. And while she does, she has found time to pray like she hasn't had for years.

My mother-in-law recently quit smoking after several decades and started walking at least a mile a day after a mild heart attack scare. If we are to redeem the time that God has given us and use it for Him, one of the best things we can do is to ensure that our bad habits won't cut our time short. Besides, the more we exercise, the more energy we'll have for sex anyway! As we start to exercise, too, we actually pay attention to our bodies. Instead of ignoring them, we treat them like friends, which opens the door to letting our sexuality shine through.

Your Body—Your Friend

Do you like your body? I don't mean do you think you're attractive, I mean do you like it? Think of what an amazing thing it is. It breathes on its own. It gives you energy, has babies, cools you down, warms you up, digests food. It allows you to hug, to laugh, and to run. Your body can do wonderful things, whether or not it lives up to some aesthetic ideal.

When we feel overweight or ugly and hate our bodies, all too often we become disconnected from them. We're not "in touch" with what they're feeling, because if we pay attention to them we're reminded of our failures. It's as if we're going through life just like squabbling children, yelling, "I'm not listening! I'm not listening!" We don't listen to our bodies' cues.

No wonder we suffer from lower sex drives! We're not used to paying attention to what our bodies want. As we start exercising, though, our whole attitude can change. We're forced to notice how our bodies are feeling. "I'm awfully tired!" our lungs might cry. "AAAAGGHH!" our stomachs might echo the day after we attempted sit-ups for the first time this millennium. But it's a good "AAAAGGHH!" Muscles actually like to be worked. It hurts, but it's a satisfying feeling.

As we start to experience these new sensations, we turn our internal sensors back on. In so doing, we can begin to tune in to our natural sex drives. Exercise sets the stage for us to listen to what our bodies want. Our attitudes shift so that our bodies aren't sources of shame anymore, but are our allies. Once we start exercising, or stretching, or lifting small weights, we have to listen to our bodies. We begin to understand how our bodies can be our friends.

When you have a friend, you nurture that relationship by talking and listening. Let's do the same for our bodies. Many of us begin our mornings trying to jolt our minds awake with coffee. Let's jolt our bodies, too, but in a kind way. Take a brisk walk, even just for five minutes. Stretch. Do sit-ups. This doesn't need to be onerous, but begin the day by *feeling*—even if it's feeling your lungs work—and you'll be more inclined to want to end it by feeling, too.

Your body is your friend, your best ally in this life. If we aim to live a healthy lifestyle and treat our bodies well, we're not focused on body image or self-acceptance, but on living out God's best. "By embracing a life of self-care—eating well, exercising, getting restful sleep, taking time out," Pam Smith explains, "we can rise up to our calling."[6] We'll stop feeling miserable about how we look, and instead we'll feel confident, comfortable, and in touch with the bodies God gave us. And when we're comfortable in them, chances are we'll be eager to see how much more they can actually do!

For Him

Most women hate their bodies. Perhaps you find that hard to understand, because you look at your wife and she looks good to you. But if she's not what she thinks is perfect, she's likely feeling really guilty. Little brings out guilt more in a woman than feeling like she has no self-control and can't lose weight. It's a character issue to her, far more than it is just a beauty issue.

Remind her that she is important because of how God made her, and tell her repeatedly what you find beautiful about her. This kind of reinforcement can help her. Also, help her to focus on being healthy rather than on losing weight. Exercise with her. Talk about changing your diet so it's healthy, too. If she's trying to punish her body with crazy diets, gently tell her that you'd rather she be healthy, even if it takes longer to lose weight.

Finally, never, ever mention how beautiful you think another woman is, even just in passing. Save all your compliments for her, and she may start believing them!

Chapter 9

Light My Fire!

It's the moment we've all been waiting for! We've demolished all those obstacles to a healthy sex life (or at least we have a plan to minimize them), and there's nothing else standing in our way. But even the best plans run into trouble. Marriages are lifelong commitments, and strategies that work at one point in your marriage may not work at others. So in this final chapter, we will look together at common scenarios that can hinder a fun sex life and see how we might deal with them. This chapter is written for you to return to again and again throughout your marriage as you go through different challenges. Some of these themes are covered in other parts of this book, while some are new. If there's a scenario that applies specifically to you, ask your husband to read that section, too, so you can discuss it together. (He may want to read this whole chapter with you!) Finally, I touch briefly here on some of the most common technique problems. If you need further help in these areas, please refer to the resources section at the end of the book.

When You Don't Feel Like It

Maybe you've read through this book and you're committed to being generous to your spouse. You even want to begin to really enjoy lovemaking! You just wish your desire was more in line with your convictions. We've talked about this throughout the book, but here are a few more suggestions to get you started.

Let God In

God cares about our sex lives. We may know that in our heads, but sex is not something we naturally take to God. It should be. Sex is the picture of God's intimate relationship with us, and He uses it to build bonds between two people. That's why prayer is one of the best tools we have for switching on our libidos. After all, God wants to give good things to us (Luke 11:13), so He wants us to have a physically pleasurable marriage.

But prayer helps in another way, too. The more on fire we are for God, the more on fire we will be for life. Before we knew Christ, it was as if we were the walking dead. When we accepted Him, we were made alive. It's similar to how you feel after you get over a cold and food suddenly has flavor. You don't realize what you are missing until suddenly you can breathe.

When we get closer to Jesus, we feel more intensely alive. We feel passion: passion for the lost, passion for life, even passion for our husbands. In fact, that's how it works. Our spirituality and our sexuality are interconnected, because both are so close to the center of our being. If you want passion for your husband, then you also need passion for life, and thus passion for God. Perhaps this is one reason that highly religious people tend to have better sex lives.[1] When both our spirituality and our sexuality are redeemed, passion flows.

Jump In

If we want to increase the excitement factor in our marriages, often all we have to do is decide to. Yet making a decision to feel a certain feeling does seem bizarre. Aren't feelings supposed to occur spontaneously? Feelings, though, are formed from a variety of stimuli. When soldiers in World War I were wounded, many times they didn't feel pain; they felt euphoria. They were finally going home! The horror of what they had already experienced changed something extremely traumatic into something liberating. Similarly, our feelings are not just random. They're influenced by our experiences and how we choose to interpret them. Deciding to feel excited doesn't rob sex of its spontaneity. Instead, it's simply reinterpreting how we view sex.

One of the biggest libido killers, especially for women, is indecision. Because we women need our heads in gear before our bodies follow, we tend to consult our feelings to decide if we want to make love. *Am I in the mood?* we wonder. Yet as soon as the question enters our consciousness, all the reasons why we *shouldn't* be in the mood are up for debate.

If your husband wants sex every single night, and seems oblivious to your legitimate feelings, I am not suggesting that you have to say yes every time. But if there isn't an overarching reason, decide to enjoy yourself. Dr. William Cutrer has found that when counseling married couples, this decision makes all the difference. He says,

> For the typical woman, getting aroused sometimes is more a decision than a product of stimulation by her husband. If she has decided she is uninterested, caressing her body will probably annoy her. If she has decided "yes," the same stimulation will usually arouse her.[2]

It sounds revolutionary, but try to stop asking yourself about your feelings and tell yourself what you want to experience. Just like those soldiers, you can influence how you feel by being careful how you think. Philippians 4 tells us to deliberately think about things that help our relationship with God—and I think that should include thinking about our husbands! So don't surrender yourself to introspection; take a leap and change your thought patterns. If it sounds impossible, decide to try it, just for tonight, and see what happens!

Nurture Great Expectations

Shortly before my wedding, my mother and I took a shopping trip where a store name caught my eye—Great Expectations. Being a soon-to-be bride, I naturally assumed this was a lingerie store. I was rather disappointed, and a little embarrassed, to see maternity jeans in the window.

When it comes to sex we need great expectations. But for Christians, thinking about sex can be a minefield. We want to be enthusiastic about making love, but we must also steer clear of all the harmful sexual imagery in society.

Being too eager to maintain purity, though, can also be potentially harmful. Lori, thirty-nine, finds one of her biggest challenges is finding safe ways to think about sex. "I find I'm constantly turning away from images that are sinful, like the covers of magazines or lingerie stores. I spend my life trying to tune out these messages. Sometimes that makes it very hard to turn on when I do want to!"

According to Ginger Kolbaba, the managing editor of Christianity Today International's *Marriage Partnership* magazine, many women suffer from Lori's problem, but many more suffer from the opposite one. As we saw earlier, when we internalize society's sexuality, married sex stops being exciting. It's too tame. I believe we can find a safe medium, although it's an awfully fine line. The answer is to dwell on what is good and pure.

The amount that "good" and "pure" encompasses might surprise you. Read Song of Songs and look at how graphically the lovers talked about each other. He praises her lips, her hair, her face, her neck, her breasts, her beauty. She invites him to enjoy her, to taste her, to drink his fill of love. And then they both talk very explicitly about how they enjoy making love. She says, "His fruit is sweet to my taste," and he talks about wanting to enjoy everything about her. They hold nothing back, either in their admiration or their excitement.

What do you admire about your husband? Perhaps like Solomon's lover, not all the attributes are physical. She likes his strength and power. What qualities make you salivate? His strength? His hands? Perhaps it's something that shows you how well you fit together. I remember something beautiful my friend Paul once related about his wife, Judith. Born with cerebral palsy, Judith walks with a pronounced limp, something most people would find bothersome. But Paul, who has poor eyesight, says the limp helps him see Judith from a distance. "When she's walking in a group, I can always find her. I know she's there." Their weaknesses actually combine beautifully to show how they were perfectly designed for each together. And you can tell how crazy they are about each other just by watching them!

Make a list of all the things that do excite you and remind you how lucky you are. It may sound odd, but the process of actually listing these things helps you to realize how sexy he really is to you. And you're more likely to remember them all, too, if you've had the experience of writing them down. It's okay to get as graphic as you want, too! You are, after all, married. You have the ultimate permission slip, so you may as well use it for fun.

Don't stop at his attributes that you find exciting; think, too, about what you have done in the past that you really enjoyed. Give yourself some safe but fun images to fill your mind, so that instead of turning away from sex entirely when *Cosmo* comes into view, as Lori does, you can play your own perfectly legal tape in your head instead. A great exercise to awaken both your pulses is to share this tape with him and ask him to tell you what memories he cherishes.

Our mind is our biggest sex organ, but too often it doesn't get used that way. When we're passive, allowing what's outside of us to dictate our thoughts, very often what's outside of us also dictates our feelings. Dream of your husband at specific times throughout the day, like every time you're in the shower, when you're blow drying your hair, or when you're doing the dishes. Get in the habit of thinking about him and smiling, because you have a special secret that only he's privy to.

As you start to think about these things more frequently, in a positive context, you're likely to find that the patterns your mind takes are purer. You won't cater to inappropriate fantasies anymore, but you will think about sex! That's how you turn up the heat.

Dare Yourself to Make Him Feel Great

Sometimes one reason we may not feel in the mood is that we're concentrating on how we feel. But sex is also about giving, and making one's spouse's toes curl can be fun in and of itself. Dare yourself to make your husband feel great. Give him an incredible time, regardless of what happens with you. Men report that what they really value is enthusiasm. One man whose wife rarely made love explained it this way:

> If us high-desire spouses have to ask for sex every time, then we are back to feeling like we are children begging the Mommies for candy at the candy store (and *we all* hate this). True love requires that the wife seek sex from her husband. If you do not seek sex from your husband, the message you are sending is that of rejection of him whether you meant to or not.[3]

Be enthusiastic about sex and you speak his language. Afterward, even if the mountains don't move for you, he'll feel much more relaxed, you'll have more self-confidence, and likely you'll find yourself aroused just seeing what you can do to him!

Reasons You Might Not Feel Like It

"I Lose My Libido at Certain Times of the Year"

Our unconscious memories are long, and often when an intensely negative emotion is felt during a certain season, we'll feel that depression, grief, or fear every year at that same time, even if we're not consciously thinking of the trauma.

My son was diagnosed with a fatal heart condition in utero in April 1996, and he died that September. For years afterward, my husband and I would have wonderful winters together, only to hit a brick wall when spring arrived.

If you or your husband lose your libido suddenly, see if it's near the date of a traumatic event, like the death of a close family member or the anniversary of an accident, a divorce, or depression. This knowledge may not alleviate the grief or the problem, but it does help you both understand it. Pray for healing for the trauma and support each other through it. Likely, with time, the effects will lessen.

"I Don't Find My Husband Sexually Attractive"

With the rates of obesity increasing so quickly, many of our husbands resemble Fred Flintstone far more than they do Tom Cruise. Can we get excited by Fred Flintstone?

Julie had this problem with her husband, Brian. When they married, Brian was already a large man, though not overweight. Yet while Julie spent the next few years having four babies and maintaining her weight close to what it had been pre-pregnancy, Brian ballooned.

Julie began to feel cheated. She was trying to stay attractive for him, but he was doing nothing for her. And quite frankly, as he ballooned to over two hundred pounds, sex was no longer as exciting or even as comfortable as it had been before. Julie is a common sense type of woman, and when she sees a problem, she expects it to be fixed. So she sat Brian down and told him lovingly but firmly that their marriage was one of the most important things in her life, but she admitted, "Honestly, honey, you just don't turn me on anymore. And that really saddens me."

Brian took it to heart, and to Julie's joy and surprise he joined a gym, changed his eating habits, and started to shed pounds. It took two years for him to reach his target weight, and he actually weighs considerably less now than when they married. Julie says now, "When he comes into a room he literally takes my breath away. And he knows it!"

Julie and Brian took a long time to find this new equilibrium, and perhaps your spouse is not as enthusiastic about a gym membership as Brian was. For women, this is where sex being primarily in our heads really comes in handy—we can usually think our way out of it. If you focus on some of the things you've written down about him that do excite you, you take the focus off the fact that he may not be pin-up material.

If you want things to change, talk to him about it gently. Let him know that you're worried about your sex life, and you're worried about his health. Try not to sound condemning or as if you're rejecting him, since nothing can be harder on a man than to feel as if his wife thinks he's not sexy. But perhaps a heart to heart talk, like the kind Julie had with Brian, is just what your marriage needs to become more highly charged!

If you are the primary cook in the family, though, you have great powers (especially if you also do the grocery shopping)! Get rid of needless starches, like breads, cakes, or potatoes, and focus on healthy food. There's no reason he even needs to know it's healthy, given all the wonderful things you can cook with virtually no fat but tons of flavor.

Finally, make exercise fun for the whole family. Go on walks together, take up biking, or learn a winter sport that can burn some calories. Don't make exercise into a chore your husband has to do alone. Are there some sports that he does enjoy, like squash, or soccer, or baseball? Encourage him to join a team or league. Our church has a hockey team, and even though my friend Bruce is already really busy, his wife Tanya wants him to go and have fun and exercise. If he keeps it up, Bruce won't have a pot belly in ten years like many men do in their forties.

"I Have to Fantasize to Get Excited"

As we talked about in chapter 4, many who have dabbled in pornography or who have promiscuous pasts can find married sex too tame, and have to fantasize about something else in order to get excited. They can't "be there" when they're making love. Reread chapter 4 to see the background of this problem and how you can start to deal with it.

Here are some additional suggestions. Remember that fantasy is not okay, even if you're still being intimate with your husband. You are committing adultery in your mind. Fantasizing about your husband and what you've done in the past is fine. It's a shared experience. Marnie Ferree, who helps people recover from sexual addiction, says anything else is not.

Embracing a pure sexuality can be a long process, but healing of the initial trauma can help. If you deliberately sought out pornography, repent of that. But many of us sought it out because we were already broken. Most sex addicts are abuse survivors, and that abuse can mar our sexuality. As you start to heal this initial trauma, the need for the fantasies will diminish.

If you are addicted to fantasies, even if you don't use pornography, you still need to break free, in the same way that an alcoholic needs to give up drinking altogether. You can't just have a small glass of wine every now and then. You need to become sober. As hard as it is, let your husband know about the struggles you are having. When you're making love and the fantasies return, tell him you have to stop. Don't bring fantasies into your marriage bed again, even if it means you don't have an orgasm for a while. Just enjoy sex with him. Try making love with the lights on, too, so that you can be sure to be "present," looking him in the eye and kissing him. That reminds you who you're with and what you're supposed to be doing!

"My Husband Never Wants to Make Love!"

The day may come when your husband, who was all over you when he was twenty-four, seems ambivalent. You want to reignite your sex life to give some vitality to your marriage, but he doesn't seem to be a willing partner. You're not alone. In one-third of marriages, it's women on the losing end, not men, especially as couples age.[4] This presents a more complicated problem: when you're not in the mood, you can still make love. Anatomically, it just doesn't work if he's not interested.

In some cases, though, this may be because you haven't tried. Most of us marry at a stage in our lives when he has the higher sex drive, and when kids follow, this pattern can last a decade or even longer. During that period, many of us fall into routines, one of which may be that he usually initiates sex. In periods of stress, or as he ages and the urge isn't as intense, his sexual energy may be channeled elsewhere and he may stop.

That does not necessarily mean, though, that he can't enjoy sex or become excited; it's just that he doesn't need it now to the same degree that he once did. If you turn it up a notch, you may be able to entice him. Doing so can also do wonders for your husband's sexual confidence, because he realizes you find him desirable, especially at a time in his life when he is under great stress and needs that affirmation.

One of the best ways to entice a man is to play to his eyes. Men like to see things, even those things we women might rather keep hidden. Coming from a cold climate, this isn't the easiest thing in the world for me for at least seven months of the year. My husband likes to keep the nighttime temperature of our house around 65, and believe me, no one wants to be dressed skimpily at 65 degrees. So tell him that if he wants to turn up the heat in the bedroom, he needs to turn it up in the rest of the house! Keep your thermostat up occasionally when you're planning a nice evening, or move a small space heater into the room. Consider having a hot bath, too; the warm water increases blood flow and makes you feel warmer even afterward.

If your problem isn't goose bumps as much as it is fat rolls, take heart! Silky clothes are available in every size now, and you may actually feel more sexually confident in a nice negligee than you would naked (and chances are he'll like it, too!). You don't have to buy something that makes you look like a prostitute, but you should show at least a little skin. The key to sexiness is maintaining a little mystery (that's why a little bit of lingerie is sexier than absolute nakedness). But a lot of mystery can be too much! I have a flannel nightgown that my husband likes to joke must be the sexiest thing in the world, since it leaves absolutely *everything* to the imagination. But in reality this "nightgown of mystery" is hardly sexy. If your wardrobe consists mostly of flannel, you may need to consider a shopping trip.

If your husband's sex drive is not just diminished, but seems to be in permanent deep freeze, consider seeing a Christian counselor yourself and asking what steps you can take to encourage your husband to get help. Pick someone you're comfortable with and who has experience in this area, or turn to the resources section following this chapter for more ideas.

"My Husband Has Problems Maintaining an Erection"

Many men lose desire because they lose confidence. Even though we women are the ones who usually decide the if and the when of sex, men decide when we start and often, though not always, when we stop. A man's ability to maintain an erection is much more intrinsic to the sex act than is his wife's ability to be excited. Losing an erection can be psychologically devastating.

Do not overreact or belittle him in any way. Even too much compassion can be dangerous for men, for then we're not treating them like "manly males," but almost like children who need to be comforted. That's the last thing they want at that time.

The most likely cause of impotence is fairly easy to treat, anyway. It's usually health related. Impotence could be a sign that your husband is developing diabetes or high blood pressure, so a visit to the doctor is always in order. It's a very common side effect of many medications as well, a fact that doctors may fail to warn patients about when they scribble the prescription down.

If it isn't medical, it's psychological. Often it can be due to stress at work, and your husband may just need some space to work it out. If it's a problem in your relationship, follow some of the other steps in this book to try to build intimacy. But above all, don't allow the problem to blow up out of proportion. Most men experience it at some point, it is usually temporary, and there's no reason to think that a fun sex life can't resume soon.

"It's Too Predictable"

When you're first married, everything is new and exciting. It's like you're a kid set loose in the candy store. But that excitement inevitably diminishes. Part of the excitement is the unknown.

TV sitcoms illustrate this perfectly. Many of them took ratings dives once the two main characters finally hooked up. Think Sam and Diane on *Cheers,* or Tony and Angela on *Who's the Boss.* It's the tension that's exciting and that keeps us coming back for more. When we've been making love for fifteen years on the same bed at the same time each day, that tension can evaporate, even if sex still feels good. Of course, there's no need to make major changes in your sex life unless you want to; there's nothing wrong with a predictable sex life, and if you're both happy, then rejoice!

Sometimes, though, especially when you have the lower desire level, rituals can spell trouble. If he always kisses deeply when he wants to make love, you may start avoiding all deep kisses—even though you like them—because you're reluctant to go further.

Shake it up a little bit, though, and you avoid these problems. Try somewhere else just for variety. Consider going out to a hotel for a night, or swap baby-sitting with another couple so you have the whole house to yourselves, and try rooms other than the bedroom. There's nothing wrong with making love at other times of the day, too. Be spontaneous. Stay in bed an extra ten minutes for a quick intimate encounter (just keep the door locked if you have kids). Or grab a quick shower together. While dragging out romantic interludes can be fun, short ones can also be exciting. If you keep up this kind of spontaneity, you restore some of that tension that you first had in your marriage. No one knows what's coming next.

"We Never Have Any Privacy!"

In a study done by Paul Pearsall, one woman stressed the importance of privacy this way: "If you're not careful, [kids] will take custody of your marriage." She explained that their marriage had gone through plenty of Vaseline—rubbed on their doorknob so little hands couldn't turn it.[5] Instead of raising children, Pearsall claims, we should raise families, and that means protecting the marriage from harm the kids can cause.

Teach your children to respect your privacy. My six-year-old can pick the lock on our bedroom door with surprising ease. I think she has a future in law enforcement (at least I hope it's on that side of the law). We've had to teach her that if the door is locked it's for a reason. She needs to knock, and we will always come and get her.

Privacy also means minimizing the chance your children will need you. Giving children set bedtimes is one of the best things you can do for your sex life, to ensure that you have time alone together at night. When kids are older, consider setting a time that they have to be in their rooms, even if they're not sleeping.

Carrie, a friend of mine with teenagers, says a radio also works wonders for privacy. She and her husband share a small house with their three children, with bedrooms jammed close together. Now that their children stay up as late as if not later than they do, the fear of children overhearing can easily kill the mood. Click on the radio, and you give yourself some more privacy. And remember, it will get better. Susan, fifty, says that was the greatest thing about being an empty-nester. She misses her kids, but now she and her husband's sex life is much more spontaneous!

"We've Been Away from Each Other So Long"

My friend Suzanne's husband was posted in the Middle East last year for six months, and needless to say, both were looking forward to being together again. Her advice? Don't build up the reunion too much in your mind. Don't think, "I'll come into the room wearing this, and then he'll say that," and have it all planned out. It won't happen that way and you'll just be disappointed. Instead, give yourself time to just be in the moment and get reacquainted. It's wonderful if the fireworks happen (and Suzanne swears they did), but it's so much easier if you don't put a lot of pressure on yourself.

Suzanne also urges us to remember that part of lovemaking after a long absence is making up for all the insecurities about your relationship you inevitably faced when you were apart. Take time to show each other how much you do love each other. Perhaps you want to have a long talk and reassure each other verbally and with tender affection before you move on to the lovemaking. But then again, I'm a woman. I'm not sure if a man who has been in the desert—in more ways than one—would see it the same way. It may not seem romantic, but my advice would be to welcome him home enthusiastically, if you can manage it. He's much more likely to be able to give you the affirmation you need after he feels more relaxed.

On the other hand, what if the absence hasn't been six months, but only six days, and during that time you've had to deal with multiple crises while he's had his evenings to himself in a comfortable hotel room? You may not feel very generous towards him right now. Try to analyze your frustration. Is it necessarily his fault, or do you just need a break? If it's the latter, see if you can work out a plan to find time to yourself while he is home. That may help you to feel more generous towards him now, when he needs it most! If these absences are frequent and are affecting your marriage or your children, see if you can change your lifestyle. If it's not a case of national security, perhaps you can find a way to travel together, or to limit the amount of traveling either he or you has to do in the future.

Hormonal Problems

"Right Before My Period I Just Don't Feel Sexy"

Many women find that their sex drives are far more determined by the time of the month than by anything else. Chart yourself for a month or two and find out if this is the case with you. Do you consistently feel in the mood the week after your period, but lose that feeling fairly quickly? Believe it or not, you can use this calendar to your advantage.

Chances are that for several days a month you *are* in the mood. But what if on those days you plan a heavy day of errands, and by the time nighttime rolls around you're exhausted? Or what if that's the night you choose to invite a group of friends over for dinner? It won't matter how much you're in the mood, you likely will be too tired or won't have opportunity.

Schedule in when you think you're going to be interested in sex. It may take a few months of charting to establish a pattern, but most likely you will be able to find one. On those days, make sure that you don't book yourselves too heavily. Perhaps make an extra effort to make a nice dinner for two after the kids go to bed, or, if your kids are older, once they're settled doing their own thing. Socialize with others on nights when you know you won't be making love anyway. That way you still have fun, relaxing together building your relationship in other ways, and you have time to concentrate on the physical side when your body is more ready and eager for it.

"I Have a New Baby and I Don't Want Anyone Else Hanging on Me"

Making love after childbirth can be a challenge, especially if you're also breastfeeding. When women become excited, they can leak milk, something that can quickly cut desire.

A simple way around this is to feed the baby before you make love. Try to get into a pattern in which the baby is fed around 9 P.M., and then when it's time to be intimate, your breasts are far less likely to leak. You can even pump after feeding to make sure you're empty, and then you may not feel the physical reminder of the baby at the exact time when he or she is the last thing you want to be thinking about!

Parenthood can also cut his desire. Some men react to seeing their wives give birth in ways that might surprise us. Seeing their wives' pain, especially if it was a dangerous or difficult delivery, may make men turn off sex for a while out of guilt. Talking to him and taking some of the steps mentioned above to ignite his sex drive should calm his fears.

Other men have problems thinking of her as anything other than "mommy." Trace Adkins may sing "One Hot Momma," expressing how desirable he finds his wife, but that's not the way your husband reacts. The best remedy is to make sure that for several nights a month you are not just mommy. Hire a baby-sitter and get away from the house. Make an effort to put away the sweat pants and comfy "mommy" clothes and dress like a woman. Then, when you are alone, don't act like "mommy," but act like "lover." Try not to talk only about the children, and don't fret about them. Remind him—and yourself—of who you were before the children came along, because one day you will be that couple again.

"I Don't Want to Get Pregnant"

When several toddlers are underfoot, or you're starting to hit forty, the thought of another baby can make sex seem far too risky. And the birth control methods that are most effective and the least messy don't work for everyone. The birth control pill, for instance, can play havoc with some women's moods and make their sex drives disappear. If you're having problems like this, check with your doctor, because another formulation may work better. If you can't use the pill at all, or aren't comfortable with it for other reasons, talk to your doctor about other alternatives. Many men balk at condoms, but comparison shopping may help you identify a brand that gives him more sensation, making him more inclined to use them. If he still seems reticent, and condoms seem the best choice in your situation, explain to him in as sultry a voice as possible that he's likely to get more lovin' if he agrees to wear one. Otherwise, it's too nerve-wracking for you!

A vasectomy is the ultimate form of birth control (and much easier, quicker, and safer than the female equivalent), but it's a decision not to be rushed. If you have several toddlers now and you're exhausted, it's easy to think your family is done. But five years from now, when you're still young enough for kids, you may find yourself pining for the other babies you could have had. Vasectomies are reversible, but there is no guarantee that a reversal will work.

If a vasectomy is out of the picture, and birth control seems messy, try playing the calendar game again. When we try to get pregnant, we plot on the calendar the days when we're most likely to be fertile. But this can work in reverse as well. Women tend to be most fertile on days 11–16, counting the first day of our period as 1. On other days, if our cycle is regular, it's virtually impossible to get pregnant. "Virtually" impossible, though, doesn't mean absolutely impossible! My husband says that in medical circles, they have a word for those who practice natural family planning. It's *parents*. One reason is that all our cycles are not necessarily regular. Travel, being in close proximity to other women, or other factors may cause us to ovulate unexpectedly early or late. You can, however, combine two methods of birth control, making it less likely that you will get pregnant. Use condoms on the days that pregnancy is more likely, and do without, if you would rather, on the other days. Nevertheless, this obviously isn't foolproof. There isn't a way to reduce the risk to zero, and that's something that we will just have to accept, knowing that any baby that does come along will always be precious and planned by God.

"I'm Hitting Menopause and My Sex Drive Is Disappearing"

Menopause doesn't suddenly happen; our bodies build up to it for several years, and one third of women find their desire decreasing during this period. Once menopause hits full force, that number increases to 40 percent.[6] This is due to a number of factors, but one is that our bodies stop producing as much testosterone. Talk to your doctor about testosterone boosts if you feel you would benefit.

Two other things that are likely to help include exercise, which keeps us more energetic and the blood flowing to those parts of the body where we want the excitement, and using lubricating jelly. Women sometimes have a harder time lubricating once they hit menopause, making intercourse painful. Use jelly, and you take away this problem and may find that you enjoy it again.

Some women actually find their sex drives increase after menopause because they're free! After menopause you can have sex every day of the month with no mess, no fuss, and no worry. Let your imagination run wild with all the new possibilities, and your libido might just perk up!

Tug of War

"He Thinks We Never Make Love Even When We Do!"

My friend Lori once quipped to me that two minutes after they had made love, her husband could turn to her and lament, "We haven't had sex in three weeks!" It doesn't matter how much he enjoys it, he always feels like he wants more and forgets what just happened.

I recounted this story to my husband, who laughed and said, "So I'm not the only one!" Then he made me promise, "Tell your readers that that's *all* I got out of that story!" In other words, he's sure he's never going to gain an accurate perspective on the frequency of lovemaking because he's a guy, and his default setting will always be "more."

When men feel like they need physical release, they will interpret that to mean that they haven't had sex for ages—even if it was just two nights ago. If a man is expecting to make love, his body gears up for it all day. It won't matter if you made love just last night, if you say no he will still feel physically frustrated and may act like he hasn't had sex forever.

One way to counteract this is to talk about sex afterward. Call him at work the next day and whisper what you liked best about last night. Remind him that you did actually make love, and he's less likely to assume you're withholding (although more likely to dream of a repeat performance!). Another strategy is to schedule sex. This may seem very unromantic, and each encounter certainly doesn't have to be scheduled, but if you schedule a special date regularly, at least he knows that you are making love with great intensity on a frequent basis.

"All We Do Is Fight over Sex"

Sometimes sex becomes so full of conflict that you need a break to gain perspective on your relationship. A hiatus can provide the space you need to build the relationship so sex becomes a more natural expression of how you feel about each other.

When Debbie, a youth minister, got married, she was worried about her sex life with her husband, Matt. On reaching puberty, she had been repeatedly fondled by her father. She soon found that her body tensed up at the thought of anything sexual. She couldn't insert a tampon, and she had to stop the doctor from performing an internal exam because it was too painful. She prayed that her wedding night would be different, but it was not.

Debbie had vaginismus, or an involuntary tightening of the vaginal muscles near the opening, making sex very painful. Debbie was devastated, and Matt probably was too, but knowing her story he just held her. After a few months of tender affection, Debbie found that she trusted him enough that her body started responding. She could actually make love.

The benefits of a break aren't just for those who are having physical problems, but also for those for whom sex has become too ridden with conflict. If he's willing, explain that having him hold you for a few weeks, or days, or whatever you both can manage, can help you to feel that he loves you, regardless of what you do. Sometimes women need to reestablish this trust before they can move forward to a great sex life. Remember the instruction that Paul gave in 1 Corinthians 7, though. This break is not to be perpetual, or even too lengthy, and is only to be taken if both parties consent.

You can also take a "sexy" hiatus from sex! When women feel pressured into having sex, we can sometimes lose track of what we desire because we're always reacting to him. We don't know what feels good, or even what we want, because we haven't had a chance to figure it out. We're always focusing on the end goal—his release—so he feels better.

Try taking a week, or even just a night, when you are free to explore his body without having sex afterward. Remove the pressure, and you may find your own desire awakening. You don't have to worry about what's coming, about whether you're in the mood, or about whether he's going to be angry. You can just do all the other things you've dreamed of. Maybe that's actually just kissing. Maybe you just need to feel affection with no strings attached. Knowing that he can give that to you—that he still loves you apart from your sexual relationship—builds confidence and trust.

"He Says I Have Too Much Power over Our Sex Life"

In most marriages the woman is the one to determine the frequency and timing of sex. He'll always want to; she's the one who may say no. This situation can leave men feeling powerless, since women seem to hold the veto over what's one of the most important things to them.

David and Leslie had been struggling with this for years. They had a healthy sex life, but he felt that she was always the one to decide the when and the where. David was getting frustrated. He was willing to agree not to pressure her, but it was very difficult. So for Christmas one year, Leslie gave him twelve coupons, redeemable for great sex when she wouldn't just lie there, but would be a willing partner. He could hold onto them and use one a month, waiting for the night when he needed it most.

Surprisingly, he didn't end up using them. Just knowing that he had them was enough to lessen his stress. He didn't have to worry that he was going to go without sex forevermore (an unrealistic concern if you looked at their marriage objectively, but very real to David nonetheless), and so he could wait until a particularly desperate time to use them. He started to realize that he wasn't actually as desperate as he thought. Allowing him to have the upper hand, so to speak, allowed him to feel less helpless and nervous about their sex life. He had some control now, too.

But how was Leslie going to handle it if David had redeemed a coupon? Exactly as she promised. She says that at one stage in her marriage this would have been impossible. But as they grew together, she realized that she could be generous to him like that. It wasn't being dishonest to make love if she didn't feel like it. It was giving of herself in love, and she found that that in itself was fun.

"He's Never Satisfied!"

Sometimes we get into semantics over words. He says, "I want you to want me." She says, "But I do want to make you happy." To her, that's expressing love. To him, it's rejection. And it doesn't necessarily matter how many times they make love, he may not interpret that as meeting his needs if she is not also aroused.

It is here that the tug of war is most acutely felt. She can honestly be trying to meet his needs, but he does not interpret it that way. She wants her willingness to make love to be enough; he wants her to be enthusiastic. She feels rejected, he feels rejected, and both feel angry.

It's important to understand what men get out of lovemaking. It isn't just release. Here's how one frustrated husband explained it:

> The most important part of making love, particularly for the men, is that it *is not* about us getting pleasure, but rather the high we achieve by giving pleasure to our wives. It is our way of giving love, but when it is apparent that the person receiving our love is only there to "please" us, then it becomes rejection of us personally.[7]

It seems unfair to require women to find pleasure in sex; after all, how can we control our bodies' responses? But this is important to men's self-confidence, and we can at least make it more likely that we'll respond.

First, decide to. It doesn't matter what he does to you, if you're lying there thinking, *I wish he'd just get it over with,* you will not get excited. You need your brain in gear. Concentrate on what your body is feeling, and what you'd like it to feel. However, if he doesn't seem able to arouse you, read on!

Pleasure Problems

"He Doesn't Understand How to Touch Me"

If you're having problems becoming aroused, or if he's reached the top of the mountain when you're just starting to climb and enjoy the view, remember that sex gets better the more you have it. Men are able to "go" for longer if they don't have as much tension built up in their bodies. Making love frequently—even, at times, twice in one night—makes it more likely that sex will endure long enough that you, too, will experience pleasure. Besides, this keeps your libido out of hibernation. "Use it or lose it" applies even to sex, and if you use it, you remind your body, "See, that's what this is for!"

You also need to tell him what feels good, something that can be difficult if you're not comfortable talking about the sexual parts of your body. Yet you don't even need words. Move his hand to where you'd like it. If he does something uncomfortable, shift your body so the sensation is better. If he does something that does feel good, let him know about it. A simple "yes," or even a moan, will usually convey the message quite well.

Another thing to remember is that most women reach orgasm not because of stimulation to the vagina but because of stimulation to the clitoris. He may excite you prior to intercourse by touching, but you can make sure this excitement continues by tilting your pelvis, so that as he thrusts his pelvic bone comes into contact with your clitoris. Lying perfectly flat doesn't accomplish this. You may have been excited before you started intercourse, but the excitement soon dies off because the stimulation dies. But if you tilt slightly upward, the stimulation continues. You're also using your own muscles to squeeze the clitoral area, making yourself more ready for pleasure. When you do this, you also let him know that you're putting effort into the lovemaking process, too, and he's more likely to feel excited (and confident)!

If that doesn't work, Dr. William Cutrer and Sandra Glahn recommend putting a pillow under your buttocks to get your body in a position that's more easily stimulated. Some women also find that making love on top lets them control the level of stimulation and ensure that the couple's bodies are hitting the correct way.[8]

"I Feel Pressured to Have an Orgasm"

Many couples measure the success of their sex life in terms of whether or not she is able to achieve orgasm during sex. Unfortunately, this can be very damaging to a relationship. When women feel pressured, it's hard to respond. But it's also counterproductive for him. If she can only make love on the nights she feels she can have an orgasm, chances are the couple will make love less frequently than they would otherwise. She has to be sure she's really in the mood, or else they'll both feel like they've failed. She can't just make love to feel close to him or as a gift to him.

Don't give up the goal of mutual satisfaction; it's wonderful to want to achieve that together. Just let go of the idea that it has to happen every time. Sometimes you'll want to make love in a hurry; sometimes you'll want to drag it out. Sometimes she'll know he's had a hard day and will want to comfort him, even if she has plenty on her mind. Ironically, it's often easier to achieve orgasm if it's not the explicit goal.

"He Wants Me to Do Things I'm Not Comfortable With"

Between two married people, I think there's very little that's strictly off limits, except those things that involve fantasizing in any way about another person, whether it's through too much role playing or pornography. That being said, many of us won't want to do everything permissible, and not all of us are aroused by everything under the sun! Many things have negative connotations to us (we don't want to feel like prostitutes, for instance), and others are painful rather than pleasurable. Sex is to be a mutual experience, and it should never be done, in my opinion, if it's genuinely causing pain.

If he wants you to do something that's sinful, say no. If you think it's wrong, but he doesn't, I think the principle in Romans 14:13–23 should apply. In this passage, Paul says not to eat meat sacrificed to idols with those Christians who feel it is wrong, even though Paul himself says it's okay to do. Neither party should feel like they're sinning. Pray that he will see your point of view, and do your best to make the things that you do like red hot for him, so that he's not yearning for something else!

Sometimes, though, we think things that are perfectly fine are sinful because of our upbringing. We associate parts of our bodies with shame. If you were punished for exploring your genitals as a child, for instance, you may have an aversion to having your vagina or clitoris touched, something that is part of most people's healthy sex lives.

I heard a story third or fourth hand during graduate school about a colleague who had never seen his wife of seven years naked. She changed in the closet; locked the bathroom door; and had sex with the lights off. This story tells me two things: first, don't go to just anyone with your sexual difficulties. Gossip spreads! But second, many of us are very ashamed of things that are natural, beautiful, and part of a godly marriage. Don't be afraid to seek out a Christian counselor or a mature Christian woman you can trust to get counsel in this area. If you feel shame to this level, very likely you have some childhood trauma that you need healing from, as we talked about in chapter 4. Find a mature Christian who can pray with you and help you become freer with your husband.

Finally, if your husband wants something you don't think is necessarily wrong, but you just don't like doing it, you have a more difficult decision. You can try to do it for him, as a gift, but this can become dangerous if it starts to make you associate sex with something you dislike. On the whole, I think 1 Corinthians 7 states an attitude of mutuality in a marriage. He owns your body, but you also own his. Let's not use our bodies to hurt each other or to make each other uncomfortable. There are enough variations on the things you do like to do that you can probably spice up your love life in other ways that are enjoyable, exciting, and pleasurable for both of you!

The Last Word

Don't forget to laugh. This has been a serious book, looking at everything from childhood trauma to our body image and finding respect. But let's keep perspective: most people enjoy sex more the longer they are together. Things that seem insurmountable now most likely will not be that way in a few years. Certain times in our lives can be very stressful, especially when children are young or when they hit the teen years. But these chapters in our lives inevitably open up new chapters in which we may find new attitudes and new levels of energy we never thought possible! Love each other, seek the best for each other, and pray. You have a lifetime of fun ahead of you, and God is more than able to make up for the "years the locusts have eaten."[9]

Some Helpful Resources

Organizing Your House

Ely, Leanne. *Saving Dinner.* New York: Ballantine, 2003.

Gregoire, Sheila Wray. *To Love, Honor, and Vacuum: When You Feel More Like a Maid than a Wife and a Mother.* Grand Rapids: Kregel, 2003. Looks at two issues: how we can organize our time and priorities better so we build a comfortable home, and how we can encourage family relationships that focus on Christ at the same time.

Peel, Kathy. *The Family Manager's Everyday Survival Guide.* New York: Ballantine, 1998. Helps women organize their homes so things run like clockwork.

You can also join www.flylady.net, an online support group for organizing everything. A warning, though: if you sign up for her e-mail notices, you'll get about 20 a day and it can seem overwhelming! Some women still find it very helpful.

Recovering from Sexual Abuse

Revell, Glenda. *Glenda's Story: Led by Grace.* Lincoln, Ne.: Gateway to Joy, 1994. A personal experience story that focuses on God's grace in the healing of abuse, including sexual abuse.

VanStone, Doris, and Erwin Lutzer. *No Place to Cry: The Hurt and Healing of Sexual Abuse.* Chicago: Moody, 1990. Many have found this book, the sequel to *Dorie: The Girl Nobody Loved,* helpful in their own experience of moving into sexual healing.

Finding a Christian Counselor

Many Christian counselors are wonderful. Many, however, don't know how to handle all problems, especially sexual ones. Make sure you feel comfortable with the counselor you've chosen. To find a

Christian counselor in your area, ask your pastor for recommendations. If you don't feel comfortable doing that, phone a large church in your area and ask anonymously. Many Christian counselors also advertise in local Christian newspapers. You can also check www.aacc.net, the website for the American Association of Christian Counselors.

Focus on the Family has counselors who will talk to you on the phone for free one time. They can also help to locate Christian counselors in your area. You can call them at (719) 531-3400 during business hours.

For more information, and tips on how to interview a potential counselor, go to www.bethesdaworkshops.org, and follow the links to Resources and then to Counseling.

Questions About the Physical Aspects of Sex

If you have more questions about sex that this book doesn't cover, try some of these:

Cutrer, William, and Sandra Glahn. *Sexual Intimacy in Marriage*. Grand Rapids: Kregel, 2001.

Wheat, Ed, and Gaye Wheat. *Intended for Pleasure*. Grand Rapids: Fleming H. Revell, 1997.

Recovering from Pornography/Sexual Addiction

If you have struggles with pornography or flashbacks, or if you're married to someone who does, visit www.pureintimacy.org. It's a ministry of Focus on the Family, and has lots of articles, encouragement, and links.

If you need more help, try www.bethesdaworkshops.org. This organization helps those specifically suffering from sexual addiction, with links to counselors, seminars, articles, and online resources.

Hall, Laurie. *An Affair of the Mind*. Colorado Springs: Focus on the Family, 1998. Helps both women and men understand the devastation of pornography, and how we can overcome it.

Rogers, Henry J. *The Silent War*. Green Forest, Ark.: New Leaf Press, 2000. A chaplain shares his struggles with pornography and explains how it wrecks marriages every day. Ends with the story of a woman's heartbreak as her husband becomes more and more addicted.

Recovering from Infidelity

How do you rebuild trust in your marriage enough so that you can become intimate again? And should you? Here are some books that may help you in these struggles.

Carder, Dave, and Duncan Jaenicke. *Torn Asunder.* Northfield Publishing, 1999. The authors help people understand the causes and repercussions of extramarital affairs, giving insights into the emotions of the spouse who strays and the spouse who feels betrayed. They offer some concrete help for couples wishing to rebuild their lives after such devastation.

Dobson, James. *Love Must Be Tough.* Sisters, Ore.: Multnomah, 2004. If your spouse is having an affair, or has had affairs in the past, Dobson explains what steps you can take to save your marriage and minimize the chance that it will happen again. There are no guarantees, but Dobson offers the best advice I've found on the subject.

Endnotes

Introduction

1. William Cutrer and Sandra Glahn, *Sexual Intimacy in Marriage* (Grand Rapids: Kregel, 2001), 186.

2. Please try Christian books, because the recommendations on how to build arousal in some secular books won't help your marriage in the long run. My main suggestion would be the book by William Cutrer and Sandra Glahn, *Sexual Intimacy in Marriage* (Grand Rapids: Kregel, 2001), which covers almost all aspects of sex in great detail.

Chapter 1: He's an Alien

1. C. S. Lewis, *The Four Loves* (New York: Collins, 1960), 92.

2. Ibid., 92.

3. Courtney Beckman, "Former 'Playgirl' Editor Speaks," Indiana Statesman, 21 February 2003, at http://www.indianastatesman.com/vnews/display.v/ART/2003/02/21/3e5630b0ba574; accessed 29 December 2003.

4. "Sex Differences: What Is the Research Evidence?" Department of Psychology, Fullerton University, at http://www.psych.fullerton.edu/rlippa/gender/Gend_outline1.htm; accessed 2 September 2003.

5. If you experience some sort of pain during intercourse, talk to your doctor. One close friend of mine had an episiotomy sewn up incorrectly, resulting in pain that was easily fixed once it was diagnosed. Many of these problems, though, have more

emotional and psychological roots. Seeing a medical sex specialist is not always the best route, since he or she may medicalize the problem rather than dealing with the actual crisis that caused it. See the resource section for advice on how to find a Christian counselor. Please seek help! It doesn't have to stay this way!

6. "Sexiest Britons named in Valentine's Poll," 14 February 2002, BBC News online, at http://www.news.bbc.co.uk/1/hi/uk/1819463.stm; accessed 29 August 2003.

7. Author's name withheld, "The War Within Continues," *Leadership* 9, no. 1 (winter 1988): 24.

8. Gene A. Getz, *The Measure of a Man* (Glendale, Calif.: Regal Books, 1995), 49.

9. See Linda J. Waite and Maggie Gallagher, *The Case for Marriage* (New York: Doubleday, 2000), for a wonderful explanation of how a faithful, monogamous marriage will benefit every aspect of a woman's life.

10. Lewis, *The Four Loves*, 93.

11. G. Davey Smith, S. Frankel, J. Yarnell, "Sex and Death: Are They Related? Findings from the Caerphilly Cohort Study," *British Medical Journal* 315, no. 7123 (1997): 1641–44.

12. See James Dobson, *Love Must Be Tough* (Waco: Word, 1996), for wonderful advice on how to handle this very difficult and heartbreaking situation.

Chapter 2: Don't Worry, Be Holy

1. See Linda J. Waite and Maggie Gallagher, *The Case for Marriage* (New York: Doubleday, 2000), for a full discussion on why marriage is superior.

2. Susan McCrensky Heitler, "Pleasures of the Familiar," Radcliffe Spring Quarterly, 1998. http://www.radcliffe.edu/quarterly/199801/page16a.html.

3. For a full discussion of the implication of this on our sex lives, see C. S. Lewis, *The Four Loves* (New York: Collins, 1960), 85–86.

4. Gary L. Thomas, *Sacred Marriage* (Grand Rapids: Zondervan, 2002).

5. Sheila Wray Gregoire, *To Love, Honor, and Vacuum* (Grand Rapids: Kregel, 2003). Chapters 1 and 5 relate especially to this theme.

6. I talk about this more in chapter 5 of my book *To Love, Honor, and Vacuum.*

7. Mary Stewart VanLeeuwen, *Gender and Grace* (Downers Grove, Ill.: InterVarsity, 1990).

8. Philip Yancey, *What's So Amazing About Grace?* (Grand Rapids: Zondervan, 2002).

9. Quoted in William Cutrer and Sandra Glahn, *Sexual Intimacy in Marriage* (Grand Rapids: Kregel, 2001), 73.

Chapter 3: Heads, Shoulders, Knees, and Toes

1. Downloaded from http://www.womenshealthinthenews.net/issue4_17_2000.html; accessed 12 December 2003.

2. James Maas, *Power Sleep* (New York: Quill, 1999), 6.

3. Ibid., 8.

4. Ibid., 3.

5. See "Early to Bed and Early to Rise," press release from the Sleep Foundation, 2 April 2002, at http://www.sleepfoundation.org/NSAW/pk_celebrity.cfm; accessed 3 January 2004.

6. Richard Ferber, *Solve Your Child's Sleep Problems* (New York: Fireside, 1986).

7. Ferber's method has other aspects to it, as well. In his book, he outlines a strategy for allowing children to cry for increasingly long periods each sleep time, but still returning to the bedroom to comfort them at set intervals so they know they are loved. It's difficult for the first few days, but most parents find the crying soon stops and the children are happier.

8. "Mayo Clinic Study Is First to Scientifically Document That Bed Partners Lose an Hour of Sleep Per Night Due to Snoring Spouse," *Science Daily*, 6 October 1999, at http://www

.sciencedaily.com/releases/1999/10/991006075441.htm; accessed 4 January 2004.

9. "Sex and Exercise," at http://www.qfac.com/articles/sexercise.html; accessed 1 January 2004.

10. Ciboulette Lafleche, "Exercise Your Way to Better Sex," *Imprint*, 20, no. 16 (31 October 1997), at http://www.imprint.uwaterloo.ca/issues/103197/8Sex/sex05.shtml; accessed 1 January 2004.

11. Henry Cloud and John Townsend, *Boundaries* (Grand Rapids: Zondervan, 1992).

12. Leanne Ely, *Saving Dinner* (New York: Ballantine, 2003), xi.

Chapter 4: Throw Out That Bath Water

1. Judith Reisman, *Soft Porn Plays Hardball* (Lafayette, La.: Vital Issues Press, 1991).

2. Ibid.

3. Marnie Ferree, interview by author, personal interview, 29 December 2003. You can find more information about her and her ministry Bethesda Workshops at www.BethesdaWorkshops.org.

4. Reported by Steve Watters in "Christian Vocalist Shares Story of Struggle and Victory over Pornography," at http://www.pureintimacy.org/online1/essays/a0000027.html; accessed 17 November 2003.

5. James Dobson, introduction to Focus on the Family's Pure Intimacy Web site at http://www.pureintimacy.org/online1/; accessed 19 November 2003.

6. From Ryan Hosley and Steve Watters, "Dangers and Disappointments," at http://www.pureintimacy.org/online1/essays/a0000034.html; accessed 17 November 2003.

7. Ferree, interview.

8. Will Baude, "Virtuous Sex," blog entry at http://www.crescatsententia.org/archives/week_2003_12_14.html #002664; accessed 2 January 2004. This piece has been discussed on most major blog sites, including instapundit.com and evangelicaloutpost.com.

9. Quoted in "Cohabitation vs. Marriage," 26 Research Findings from the National Marriage Project at http://www.physiciansforlife.org/cohabitation.htm; accessed 27 December 2003.

10. As reported by Philip Elmer Dewitt, "Now the Truth About Americans and Sex," *Time*, 17 October 1994, 70, quoted in William Cutrer and Sandra Glahn, *Sexual Intimacy in Marriage* (Grand Rapids: Kregel, 2001), 207.

11. Quoted in Cutrer and Glahn, *Sexual Intimacy in Marriage*, 207.

12. An "Internet blog" is a site where people share their thoughts on recent news events. They tend to be updated frequently, and thousands are popping up every day.

13. J. P. Crawley, "Sex as Communication: The Problem with 'Pre-Sexual Marriage,'" at http://www.evangelicaloutpost.com/archives/000207.html; accessed 29 December 2003.

14. Ibid., 44.

15. For the best explanation of this that I have read, see Leanne Payne, *The Healing Presence: Curing the Soul Through Union with Christ* (Grand Rapids: Baker, 1995).

16. Leanne Payne, *Crisis in Masculinity* (Downers Grove, Ill.: InterVarsity, 1985), 56.

17. Many child sexual abuse victims feel arousal during the abuse, compounding the problem because at some level they like it. This can lead to feelings of extreme guilt and shame then, but especially later in life. See Maxine Hancock and Karen Burton Mains, *Child Sexual Abuse: A Hope for Healing* (Downers Grove, Ill.: InterVarsity, 1987), for an explanation of the effects of this.

18. Ibid., 96.

19. Ibid., 63.

20. Ferree, interview.

21. C. S. Lewis, *The Four Loves* (New York: Collins, 1960), 80.

Chapter 5: R-E-S-P-E-C-T

1. Linda Waite and Maggie Gallagher, *The Case for Marriage* (New York: Doubleday, 2000).

2. Ibid.
3. My son was born with Down's syndrome and a serious heart defect. You can read his story at www.SheilaWrayGregoire.com.
4. If you're dealing with this problem and need some more help, I highly recommend Sandra D. Wilson, *Released from Shame*, rev. ed. (Downers Grove, Ill.: InterVarsity, 2002).
5. "Study: Italian Women So Busy, No Time for Sex," at http://www.abcnews.go.com/sections/world/DailyNews/italy010813_sex.html; accessed 12 December 2003.
6. Sheila Wray Gregoire, *To Love, Honor, and Vacuum* (Grand Rapids: Kregel, 2003), 98.

Chapter 6: You Don't Bring Me Flowers

1. From Les Sillars, "Love at First Byte" *HDS Aware!* January 25, 1998, and Lorna Dueck, "The Secret of Sizzling Romance," *Crossroads Canada,* March 1999.
2. Robert and Rosemary Barnes, *Great Sexpectations* (Grand Rapids: Zondervan, 1996).

Chapter 7: Who Wears the Pants in This Family?

1. Leanne Payne, *Crisis in Masculinity* (Westchester, Ill.: Crossway, 1985), 46.
2. Quoted in ibid., 99.
3. C. S. Lewis, *The Four Loves* (New York: Collins, 1960).
4. See Leanne Payne, *The Broken Image* (Grand Rapids: Baker, 1996), for a full discussion of the erosion of the masculine gender identity in society, and its impact on homosexuality.
5. Payne, *Crisis in Masculinity,* 50.
6. Elaine Donnelly of the Center for Military Readiness has been the most vocal speaking on behalf of the children of women in combat. You can see some of these issues at http://www.cmrlink.org/womenincombat.asp.
7. From the BBC Comments page, "GCSE Results: Why Are Girls Doing Better?" at http://www.news.bbc.co.uk/1/hi/talking_point/2209280.stm; accessed 12 December 2003.

8. "Candidate Dean Declares Himself a 'Metrosexual,'" *Atlanta Journal-Constitution*, 30 October 2003, at http://www.ajc.com/news/content/news/1003/30dean.html; accessed 2 January 2004.

9. From "2003 Top Ten Campus Follies," compiled by The Young American's Foundation, at http://www.yaf.org/press/12_16_03.asp; accessed 16 December 2003.

10. See 1 Timothy 2:9.

11. See Frederica Mathewes-Green, "Let's Have More Teen Pregnancy," especially halfway through the article for a discussion on the impacts of marriage at various ages. This article appeared on National Review Online in 2003, and was downloaded from http://www.frederica.com/pro-life/more_teen_pregnancy.html; accessed 6 January 2004.

12. William Bennett, *The Broken Hearth* (New York: Doubleday, 2001).

13. See Caitlyn Flanagan, "The Wifely Duty," *Atlantic Monthly*, January–February 2003, for an overview of the novels, magazine articles, and books that discuss this trend of the "sex-starved marriage."

14. Ibid.

15. Michele Weiner Davis, *The Sex-Starved Marriage* (New York: Simon & Schuster, 2003).

16. Linda J. Waite and Maggie Gallagher, *The Case for Marriage* (New York: Doubleday, 2000), esp. 25–30, but this topic is also touched on throughout the book.

Chapter 8: Mirror, Mirror on the Wall

1. This controversy has been covered extensively by many Christian news outlets, including *Christianity Today*. For more information on founder Gwen Shamblin, visit www.christianitytoday.net and search for articles about her. An overview of the case was available at http://www.sbclife.org/Articles/2000/11/Sla7.asp and http://www.christianitytoday.com/ct/2000/138/53.0.html at the time of this printing.

2. Liz Curtis Higgs, *One Size Fits All* (Nashville: Nelson, 1993).
3. From "Poll: Most Americans Older than 25 Are Overweight," reported 5 March 2002 on CNN.com at http://www.cnn.com/2002/HEALTH/03/05/obesity.poll/index.html; accessed 12 May 2002; also from National Center for Chronic Disease Prevention and Health Promotion, "U.S. Obesity Trends 1985 to 2000."
4. Pam Smith, interview by author. 28 May 2002.
5. For a more elaborate discussion of this, see C. S. Lewis, *The Four Loves* (New York: Collins, 1960), especially the segment on eros.
6. Smith, interview.

Chapter 9: Light My Fire!

1. From Family Research Council.
2. Cutrer and Glahn, *Sexual Intimacy in Marriage*, 71.
3. Taken from a discussion board on the "Sex-Starved Marriage" at http://www.divorcebusting.com/ubbthreads/postlist.php?Cat = &Board = SEX; accessed 27 December 2003.
4. Cutrer and Glahn, *Sexual Intimacy in Marriage*, 186.
5. Paul Pearsall, *Ten Laws of Lasting Love* (New York: Simon & Schuster, 1993), 83.
6. Judith Reichman, *I'm Not in the Mood: What Every Woman Should Know About Improving Her Libido* (New York: Quill, 1999), 31.
7. Taken from a discussion board on the "Sex-Starved Marriage" at http://www.divorcebusting.com/ubbthreads/postlist.php?Cat = &Board = SEX; accessed 28 December 2003.
8. Cutrer and Glahn, *Sexual Intimacy in Marriage*, 86.
9. See Joel 2:25.

Sheila is available to speak at:

- women's conferences
- parenting conferences
- marriage enrichment seminars
- homeschooling conventions

Some of her topics include:

Hey, Honey, I Don't Have a Headache!

It's 10:00. He wants to start snuggling; you want to start snoring. Now he feels unloved because you don't want to make love; and you feel unloved because he *only* wants to make love. This seminar helps women defeat this stalemate by addressing the obstacles to our sex drive—from chores, to lack of romance, to our body image—and shows how we can overcome them to pique our sexual interest, building stronger and more intimate marriages.

Redeeming the Time

Are you always busy, but feel like you never get anywhere? It's probably because you do too many good things, and so have no time for the best! This highly practical and motivating talk will help women separate the good things they do from God's best—and learn how to focus on God's priorities even in the everyday tasks we do.

To Love, Honor, and Vacuum

If you're a mom, you're likely exhausted. This seminar helps harried women organize and prioritize, so that their lives feel less determined by the busyness of the day and more focused on the only thing that really matters: creating relationships that model Christ.

Where Is God When It Hurts?

Using her own experience overcoming abandonment as a child and the death of her son, Sheila encourages women that God will never leave. When you hurt, He hurts, too. Learn how to experience His love and peace, with a salvation message, if appropriate, at the end.

Organizing Your Homeschool

When homeschooling fails, it's often not a function of schooling. It's more often a function of family dynamics. When you're together 24/7, you can't have children who fight. You can't have an out-of-control house. You can't be distracted yourself. This seminar helps homeschooling parents create an exciting and peaceful homeschooling environment, where learning is a joy.

You can find more about Sheila's speaking at
www.SheilaWrayGregoire.com.

To Love, Honor, and Vacuum will encourage you to deal with your hectic life by prioritizing relationships and fostering responsibility and respect in all family members. When you apply these real-world, real-life insights, you'll discover what it means to love and honor . . . in spite of the vacuuming.

"Sheila is about to challenge your thinking about your role as a wife and mother. I don't say that lightly. I read more advice about mothering and womanhood in a week than most people read in a year. But Sheila is on to something here."

—Carla Barnhill
Editor, *Christian Parenting Today*

"Reading this book provides a stimulus to do practical things to make life happier for everyone."

—*Christian Observer*

"Gregoire's enthusiasm, real-life examples, and emphasis on healthy relationships will encourage women."

—*CBA Marketplace*

"Gregoire recognizes that for many women, housework isn't just housework. It's a source of deep anxiety, stress, and friction, but it doesn't have to be that way. If housework is driving you insane, you aren't alone."

—*San Diego Family*

"*To Love, Honor, and Vacuum* is full of helpful, practical ideas any mom can use."

—*Living Light News*

57810